CW00410902

ISBN-10: 978-1-3999-7150-8
Version 31-10-2023

Cover design by: Zoe Baker ©
Library of Congress Control Number: 2018675309
Printed in the United States of America

Yoursurveyors.com

MESSAGE FROM THE AUTHORS

Thank you for buying our book. This is probably one of our biggest achievements to date in our careers and we are extremely proud.

One of the main reasons for writing this is due to our many experiences of working within the property industry over the years. We realised there is very limited support and protection for people when purchasing property. We also realised homebuyers are often guided by the wrong people.

We hope that this book will provide clarity, support and guidance during what can be a stressful, emotional and expensive experience for many.

We would like to specifically thank all of our clients for trusting us over the years to carry out their surveys and valuations particularly for the many conversations we have had. We would also like to thank the owners of the properties we have inspected for being welcoming and understanding.

It is because of this that this book has been created. We have had our client's experiences good and bad at the forefront and we truly believe this will be the start of educating everyone to buy property in the right way.

All the best.

ZB & GOH
Yoursurveyors.com

CONTENTS

STOP BUYING PROPERTY
THE WRONG WAY

On average across the UK, there are around 800,000-1,000,000 property transactions per year. Our experience has shown that many of these transactions will involve people paying too much through failing to properly understand the right way to buy property. A very conservative estimate of the overspend on those transactions is in fact much more than £5,000,000,000 (five billion pounds). This is why we have produced the "The £5 Billion Homebuyer Secrets Guide".

In buying this book you may have just made the most important purchase of your entire life.

The reason we say that is because this will make sure that you go on to purchase your new home in the right way and without doubt purchasing a new home is the most expensive and significant purchase most people ever make.

We will show the way most people buy a property, which is the wrong way. More importantly we will show you the right way to buy property and in doing so expect to increase your personal wealth by typically something like £10,000 or £20,000.

We demystify the whole process of buying property.

It is presented as being relatively simple, however by not being clearly, simply, and correctly explained the purchaser often ends up making the wrong decisions whilst believing they have followed the correct and most secure pathway. They often suffer adverse financial consequences because of it. Consequences which can end up with them paying interest on a larger mortgage than they needed to have, so continuing to cost them dearly for many years into the future.

We will explain to you in a way that nobody ever does, who is on your side when buying property and who is involved in the transaction to support the seller of the property rather than the buyer. We will also explain to you many things that you have probably not considered but certainly need to know in order to buy property in the right way.

This book will not tell you how to become a property investor. There are hundreds of such books available and they are of no use to you because the great majority of potential home buyers have no interest in becoming property investors. In our experience, such books tend to be long winded and repetitious. They tend to waffle on, repeating essentially simple statements which could be summarised in a few paragraphs. What useful information they contain is expanded and repeated to fill out a book of several hundred pages, which far from lending clarity to the reader leads to confusion and increased complexity.

We believe the real reason for this is to justify charging the prospective buyer a high price for the few, simple lines of advice they often contain. Few people wish to burden themselves with all manner of different loans to buy all types of different properties which would require further expenditure to put them in a position where they may make some profit. Nor do they wish to spend years constantly turning over tenanted occupation with all the consequent risks and headaches which that brings.

As a property investor, some of your decisions will be impacted by subsequent tax implications such as the need to pay capital gains tax. Whereas when purchasing your property as your primary residence any financial gains you make are not subject to capital gains under current legislation.

The aim of this book is to give you simple messages in a straightforward manner.

Messages that you can easily understand which will reveal the secrets of purchasing a property for you to live in and will stop you making the same mistakes which many property purchasers do every time they buy property. We will show you how to save tens of thousands of pounds on your new property purchase and show you how, of course by not being a property investor you will also pay less tax.

By buying property the wrong way, most people negatively impact their financial position severely without even realising it has happened.

It is so important that you are given the right information about exactly who is on your side in the contractual arrangement of buying your new home and who is there to contractually act for the other side, and who you should take advice from and at what point you should do that.

Buying property is a contract. It involves the excitement of eventually moving into a new home, but people seem to forget that it is entirely a contractual matter. It is however an unusual contract.

Normally with a contract, purchaser A will buy something from seller B, and the arrangements between them are direct. Let's say, for example, you are buying something from a shop. In that scenario as the purchaser or customer you are client A, and the shop or seller is client B. Or let's say you are buying life insurance. Again, as the person looking to buy life insurance you are client A and the person selling the life insurance is the insurance company is client B.

In both cases, if you find after buying the product or the

insurance that there is a defect or a deficiency then as client A you can go back to the seller client B, and demand compensation, replacement or a refund depending on the circumstances.

Buying property is uniquely different from this.

In most cases when buying property, a third-party enters the direct transaction between client A and seller B. That third-party is usually an estate agent. There are many good estate agents around who do their job diligently and professionally.

Many people malign estate agents unfairly, often because they don't understand what their role is during this transaction.

However, it is very important as the purchaser that you must understand their role as a "non-independent" third-party in this transaction.

They have a duty to the only contractual client which they serve in the transaction which is client B as the person selling the property. Their duty is to achieve a sale on that property at the highest possible price and if possible, preventing anything interrupting the quick completion of the sale whatever that may be. They will be paid for this function of course by their client (client B) who is selling the property, often as a percentage commission. This means that the more the property sells for the more commission they will receive. There are some variations to this arrangement, but this is common practice and has been for many years.

This means that as the purchaser of the property (client A) you will need to make sure that you also have an independent professional acting on your behalf to assist you through this transaction or you could be left vulnerable to possibly missing information and the possibility that you could buy a property which is either overpriced or has shortcomings, legal issues, or defects.

Buying property is not like buying anything else because once you have completed the transaction there is no option for you to go and ask for a refund or a discount on whatever problems you may find later.

Under English law there is a Latin phrase which is specifically designed to cover this situation. "Caveat Emptor". This means "Buyer Beware".

When purchasing property, the Law states very clearly that if you do not take adequate advice from someone acting independently and completely on your behalf and problems arise later then it is tough luck, because you don't have an opportunity to turn the clock back.

It is imperative that you fully understand the differing relationships of the various parties involved when buying property and even more importantly, that you take correct and independent advice about the property from the right people at the right time and not from anyone whose primary duty it is to act for the other party in this transaction nor from tradesman, friends, family and others who may give well-intentioned but not professionally informed advice.

We have seen an increasing trend amongst estate agents to try and cram in as many viewings as possible for each property, especially in a buoyant market. We have noted an average time allocated for each viewing of approximately 15-20 minutes. This is certainly not enough time for the prospective buyer to see what they need for them to make a properly informed purchase decision.

That is why instructing your surveyors to act fully independently on your behalf is so important.

Your surveyor becomes your professional eyes and ears when you have not been given enough time to properly assess the property by the agent, who of course is acting in the interests of the seller only; not the buyer. Your surveyor will spend much more time thoroughly assessing the property, solely on behalf of you, the client. A purchaser can be confident the independent survey report that is prepared will be thorough and objective.

A brief time restricted viewing simply does not allow you to gather all the information you need to take a balanced and informed view on what is likely to be a life changing decision.

There are a myriad of factors to consider when buying property. Some are obvious. Most are not. The only person acting on your behalf and the most important document you can rely on is the independent survey report from yoursurveyors.com.

If on completion of a purchase you are left with a number of issues to resolve and have not taken appropriate independent advice at the right time, it would be too late to rectify that situation.

This book is designed to help stop you suffering in that way and to ensure that when you finally move into your new home, you can take comfort from the fact that you did it in the right way, ensuring protection of your future wealth, your home and your family's happiness and financial security.

WHY WE ALL BUY PROPERTY THE WRONG WAY

S o.... it is the BIGGEST purchase you will ever make in your entire life.

Even if you're a yacht buying millionaire the chances are your fancy house will still be more expensive than your yacht.

Property buying is a very personal thing. You may be looking at a modest one-bedroom flat or starter home, a classic neglected "doer upper" or a large pile in the country with stables, outbuildings and so forth. Wherever your purchase is within that spectrum it is a massive decision to make. It is a huge financial commitment of course, and property buying will impact on every single aspect of your life. The property you buy will impact not only on your financial health, but potentially, also on your physical and mental health.

Its location will impact on your daily commute to work, the schools your children can attend, your available choices of doctors and dentists, the amount of local authority charges you will pay and whether you can enjoy sitting in the garden in the summer, if you have one, or whether there are factors which will prevent this.

The wrong choice of property can impact on your personal relationships and the happiness of yourself and your family for years to come. With so much at stake it is hugely important that everybody is guided to buy a property in the correct way.

The reality though is very different and almost 100% of people buying property in the UK today, (Scotland apart), go about it in completely the wrong way.

We aim to change that and stop literally hundreds of thousands of people making bad decisions by being influenced through a process which is outdated, confusing and simply doesn't function properly to protect the consumer.

How It Works... Then And Now

One word can be used to accurately describe how the homebuying process on behalf of the consumer or buyer of property currently works. That word is "badly".

So... how does it work currently?

Initially, people inevitably get excited at the prospect of buying a new home, whether that is a first-time purchase, or they have purchased before and are looking to move to a different type or style of property, or perhaps to a different area for all manner of reasons.

Property is an exciting business. This is why there are a plethora of television programmes and magazines dedicated to property. However, what is interesting to note is that they are generally dedicated to the cosmetic appeal of property and very rarely do you actually get to understand the nitty-gritty of serious issues which can arise.

So, as a potential buyer we start from a position of excitement. Now excitement is a wonderful thing, but at times, excitement can override common sense when what is actually needed is a reality check. Never is this more important than when you are looking to buy any kind of product and do not have the technical knowledge to properly assess whether or not it is fit for purpose.

This is why laws exist in most areas of life to protect consumers.

You cannot buy an electrical appliance without it having been fully assessed as to its energy efficiency, without a set of very clear guidance instructions on how to use it and the various safety matters relating to its installation and subsequent usage.

You cannot buy a sandwich without it having been properly labelled to show you fully exactly what has gone into the making of that sandwich and in particular whether there is anything within it which could be problematic for your health.

If you are buying a car it will come with a huge multilanguage instruction manual and will have been subject to rigorous and independent safety and adequacy checks and include full details of how to maintain and service the vehicle. There is no labelling or proper instructions when you buy a property. You are the most at risk you will ever be.

Many years ago, the traditional route to finding a property would be to visit local estate agents, have a chat with them in their offices, see what they had to offer, and make an initial hopeful selection from there. Often you would take away with you sheets of property details to reflect on at your leisure. This would be supplemented by scouring through the local papers where estate agents would also advertise the various properties they had for sale.

However, the best deals were often gone by the time they had already been printed in the paper for people to view. Viewing properties would mostly be done by arranging an appointment with the current property owners. If the property was empty and the estate agent held the keys, they would meet you at the property or sometimes even drive you there from their offices. You would be able to view that property at some leisure before reflecting on a decision regarding the positives and negatives between various properties you may have inspected.

Now It Is Very Different...

Many estate agents do not have local offices today and where in the past, estate agents would only sell properties in their local area, today you will often see an agent from one town selling property in several other completely different towns. The days when people would find property from looking in the local paper or visiting estate agents' offices are largely gone.

Virtually everybody now searches for property online with sites such as Rightmove or Zoopla. The days of the leisurely considered viewing inspections for you as a potential buyer have also been predominantly superseded by agents cramming together as many viewers as possible, to suit the agents' diaries, with viewing slots usually no more than 15 minutes in length.

Yes, that's around 15 minutes to grab as much extremely limited information as you can, about making the biggest decision you will ever make which is likely to impact on your finances, your family, your work and your health for years to come.

Usually, especially in a busy market, the prospective buyer will attend several of these crammed in inspections. You will then retire to the relative safety of your own property with your family and discuss whether any of the properties you have briefly inspected are adequate to serve the purpose of becoming your home, for many years. At this point, if you decide that you do have sufficient interest in one of the properties, you will be asked to make an offer to purchase price.

However, you still have no idea of what you are actually buying and how could you?

You have been given 15 minutes for a superficial inspection of a property which has been there for 30, 50 or even 100 years or more. The property may well have had a number of different owners and they could have carried out all manner of modifications. They could have maintained the property well, or they could have neglected it. They could have undertaken works with good intent, however, it may have caused damage to parts of the building.

At this point in the transaction, unless you are that very rare buyer who is a fully qualified surveyor experienced in residential property, you would have no information on the true condition of the property you are intending to buy.

Properties are complex structures which are subject to modification and manipulation over many years, usually by people who have no professional qualification for what they do. Works undertaken inappropriately whether by under-qualified personnel or through a lack of appropriate regulatory compliance are a very common feature of properties and something we have seen numerous times.

This is the madness of the current property buying process. It allows, even encourages buyers to take on huge mortgages without first advising them to seek advice from a fully qualified surveyor before committing to a financial investment that will seriously impact on their lives for many years to come.

What Happens Next?

Once you have decided you like the prospect of a particular property; you tell the selling agent that you're interested. They will immediately want to know how much you are prepared to offer to pay for that property. Just to repeat, at this point, you have no idea of the true condition of the property, whatever its superficial appearance.

At this early stage, nobody, on your behalf, has made any actual assessment of the correct value of the property on which to base your offer. The only assessment of possible value which will have so far been placed on the property is the one at which the estate agent had been marketing. Now this may be correct, but it may also be a figure which the seller of the property hoped to achieve rather than one which was based on appropriate factors determining the value.

Estate agents have to compete against each other in order to achieve instructions. One way in which they compete is on how much they charge for selling the property and this factor can be a major influence in their decision. Another way in which they compete for business is in satisfying the potential client's aspiration of what they think their property should be worth. Human nature plays a big part here.

If four estate agents value a property and three of them suggest roughly the same marketing price but the fourth suggests a much higher marketing price and is persuasive, there is a strong likelihood that the seller of the property will instruct the agent who suggests the higher figure.

In the above example, if we consider the knowledge and experience of those agents to be on a par, by taking an average assessment of the four estate agents' valuations, the price at which the property is being marketed has been inflated.

So, along you come as a prospective buyer, keen on the property even though, as yet, you have no actual knowledge as to its true condition. You are then required to make an offer to purchase price compared against a marketing price which may well be inflated above the correct, market value. Not only according to the market, but according to an aggregate of local agents' opinions and, of course, you will not see the opinions of those agents who have not been instructed.

And so, the madness continues... Let's say that the property is being marketed at £15,000 above what most of the local agents agree should have been the correct marketing price. You decide you like the property so you make an offer, at say, £5000 below the marketing price and this gets accepted. You probably feel you have achieved a wonderful saving, whereas you are already paying £10,000 more for the property than most local agents agreed was actually a more realistic initial marketing price.

You could not be expected to realise this, how could you? After all, you have no experience of the local property market and no professional, expert advice to fall back on.

From this moment on if the seller accepts your offer to purchase price, everything becomes a hive of activity. The estate agent will want to get all your personal details. They will want to make sure you have instructed a solicitor and that you have your mortgage offer well advanced. They will want to know that you are sufficiently advanced so that the mortgage valuer, acting for the bank or building society, can be instructed to undertake a valuation on the property.

All of this costs money; Your solicitors will almost certainly want payment upfront in order to start undertaking searches. Arranging your mortgage will most likely incur charges which you will be required to pay. Often, there is a charge to cover the costs of a valuer to undertake a valuation on behalf of your bank or building society.

Before very long the costs will have mounted and yet, you still have no idea of the actual condition of the property, nor has there been an independent assessment of its value in order for you to see whether or not the price you're considering paying is correct or not.

There is a false assumption that the bank or building society valuer undertakes a survey, which they certainly do not. Bank and building society "valuers" are called that for a reason. They value the property but they do not survey the condition of the property. Neither do they assess the value on behalf of you as the purchaser but solely for the benefit of the bank or building society which has instructed them.

Another point to consider is the increasing trend nowadays, for banks and building societies to carry out what they call an AVM (automated valuation model) or "desktop" valuations, purely as a cost and time saving measure. It is highly likely that the valuation which the bank or building society carry out on the property which is specifically for their own use in assessing the suitability of the property as a security for their mortgage book, will be carried out by somebody in an office somewhere who will never visit the property at all.

There is a well-recognised parameter within the mortgage security industry that if the valuation on the property appears to be within about 5% of what might be a standard price then that will be agreed for security purposes. These parameters have been used within the mortgage security profession for many years. It means that if you are paying £400,000 for a property which on valuation assessment might be worth closer to £380,000, the valuation will probably just agree that the purchase price is within an acceptable range. The lender will not seek to advise you in any way, of what a more appropriate purchase price might actually be.

It is specifically not the job of the bank or building society valuer to advise the purchaser as to whether they are paying the correct price for the property.

Indeed, they could not realistically do this, unless they had also carried out an actual survey rather than just a valuation (especially an AVM or desktop valuation) to fully assess the condition of the various elements of the building.

So... How Should You Buy Property The Right Way?

The changes that need to be made to make sure you buy a property in the right way are in fact very straightforward, but for a variety of reasons nobody tells you these facts.

In the first instance don't allow yourself to be rushed into making the biggest financial decision of your life without having had adequate time to look at the property in question. If you are offered a 15-minute slot for an inspection, tell the agent you want two slots, because you need at least half an hour to walk around most properties and consider the various features that may or may not appeal to you. Being able to inspect properly and make a considered decision should be much more important than the agent just cramming a number of inspections into a shorter period of time, to suit their own daily timeframe.

Once you have had a decent amount of time to inspect the property and you have then gone away to discuss your findings in a more relaxed setting, it may be that you decide this property could potentially be of interest for you to purchase.

The estate agent may try to pressure you into confirming a serious interest in the property. The best way to manage this is to confirm that you are seriously interested in the property at the sale price suggested but that your final offer price will be subject to the content of your surveyor's independent survey report.

You should then proceed to instruct that survey report at the earliest opportunity.

Your surveyor's independent survey report, once prepared and forwarded to you, can then be your negotiating tool which you use to finalise an offer price on the property. If you have reservations or are uncertain about whether the initial marketing price was realistic you can include a request that the surveyor undertake a valuation on your behalf and include this in your independent surveyor's report.

As we have shown above, you cannot possibly make a sensible offer price to purchase until such time as you actually know the condition of the property, and whilst some elements of the property will be obvious to you, there will be other elements of which you will have no knowledge until such time as your surveyor's independent survey report has been carried out and sent through to you.

Remember that any valuation undertaken by the valuer acting for your bank or building society is not a valuation undertaken on your behalf, or with your specific interests in mind. This may well be carried out remotely from a desktop somewhere without any actual inspection of the property, and certainly will be without any assessment as to the detailed condition of the property as the valuers will not have undertaken a survey.

Remember that up to this point the only valuation which has been placed on the property is the one undertaken by the estate agent whose duty is to achieve the highest possible price on the sale of the property. This may or may not be reflected as a "market value", undertaken in accordance with guidance from the Royal Institution of Chartered Surveyors.

It is only after you have received and considered the content of your surveyor's independent survey report that you are actually in a position to properly make an informed offer to purchase price on the property.

Any offer to purchase made without detailed knowledge of the condition of the property would be unwise.

Experienced surveyors have expertise in identifying all manner of issues in properties which technically unqualified estate agents will have no knowledge of. Even if they did, they would not be bringing those issues to the attention of any intending purchaser. Such actions would directly conflict with their duty of care to present the property in its best possible light for their client, the vendor.

Despite living in a property for many years, it is not unusual for homeowners to be completely unaware of a multiplicity of problems. These can include; a defective roof, rising damp or potential condensation issues, boundary encroachments, subsidence, woodworm, inadequate roof structures, inappropriately formed structural openings or beams and a myriad of other things.

All of the above have the capability to financially damage the intending purchaser's wealth a long time after completion, if not properly assessed by your independent surveyor's report.

On an almost daily basis we see issues in properties, unidentified at the time of marketing, running into tens of thousands of pounds.

Purchasing a property without the information found in your surveyor's independent survey report, means that after completion of the sale, the tens of thousands of pounds possibly needed to remedy any defects will fall squarely on the shoulders of the recent purchaser. Furthermore, if this cost is included in your mortgage debt you will also be paying interest on those tens of thousands of pounds probably for 25 years or more.

There is an overarching principle of English law regarding property purchase, summarised in the Latin phrase "caveat emptor" which literally means "buyer beware". If you buy a property without obtaining an independent survey report to indicate to you it's true condition, and therefore, the correct price to be paid for it, you cannot take it back to the shop as though it were a pair of trousers which didn't fit properly.

You are simply faced with a huge bill to put things right. It would be no good complaining that the estate agent didn't market the property "warts and all" at the correct market price. Their priority is to their client, the seller of the property.

If the estate agent can complete the sale of a property without the buyers identifying issues which could have interrupted the progress or completion of that sale, and perhaps at a sale price above what the correct market value might be, then for their client, the seller of the property, that estate agent has done a very good job.

As the purchaser of property, the estate agent should not be condemned for not having your interests at the forefront of their consideration.

It is imperative that as a buyer you have a professional acting on your behalf to give you clear guidance on the condition of the property, what other actions you might need to take and the correct value at which you should proceed. Your independent surveyor's report will also give clear guidance to your legal advisors about actions they may need to carry out, on matters of which they would have no knowledge, other than through your independent surveyor's report.

Solicitors never visit the property so without guidance from your surveyors, they often have only a partial picture of enquiries they should make.

The whole property buying process in the UK (Scotland excluded as they have a different system) at the moment, specifically encourages everybody to do it in completely the wrong way.

You are given too short a time to view a property, after which you are encouraged to immediately make an offer, on the basis of no knowledge whatsoever of the condition of the property. You are, in some cases, persuaded that a building society or bank valuation is a survey of condition which it most definitely is not. You are encouraged to negotiate your final offer price, not only without professional guidance and knowledge, but in conversation with someone who has vastly more experience in that negotiation than you do, and who can best serve their client by encouraging you to pay the highest price for the property. Where estate agents are earning fees on a commission basis, they will of course earn more money if they can discourage you from negotiating the price down to a level more appropriate for yourself.

When buying property you are left very exposed to effective financial loss.

Here Is What Should Happen...

Initially, you must inform the selling agent that you need an appropriate amount of time to view the property and if they are very busy and could only offer you 15-minutes slots ask them when you can have at least 30-minutes to make a proper inspection.

Remember that there is no need for the selling agent to be there at all, if there is a vendor selling the property and the best type of inspection is one where you can have a simple straightforward conversation with the seller of the property who shows you around it themselves. Make sure you ask for that option.

Once you have viewed the property and you consider this could be one that suits your purchasing needs, advise the agent that you are interested in purchasing "at the full asking price subject to an independent survey".

Having agreed to purchase at the full asking price subject to survey, it is imperative of course that you instruct a fully independent surveyor's report on your behalf straight away. You should then explain to the agent that until you know the true condition of the property you could not finalise your offer on guesswork.

At this stage the estate agent will generally push for you to give them your solicitor's details and to start the legal processes. However, the reality is that in the vast majority of cases, if there is anything which may potentially dissuade you from purchasing the property, it is far more likely to be as a result of your surveyor's independent survey report than it is because of anything which is revealed through solicitor's enquiries and searches, even though that can happen occasionally. Given that, it is best to not immediately instruct your solicitors and start spending money unnecessarily until you know exactly what you're buying and whether you consider the offer price you will actually make, once you know its condition, is a price which the vendors will accept or not.

Instructing your solicitor will not tell you the true condition of the property. Having your mortgage valuation inspection done, will not tell you the true condition of the property.

The only way to fully assess the true condition and financial cost implications of your property purchase is to instruct your surveyors independent survey report at the earliest opportunity.

Choose your surveyors independently.

It is unlikely that you know any independent surveyors because most people only ever buy a property two or three times in their entire life. It may be that the selling agent will suggest you might use a particular company.

Some people will see value in that recommendation, although in most areas of life it is usually considered more appropriate when seeking independent advice about a purchase, not to take that advice from anybody acting on behalf of or in any way linked to the sale of the product or the seller of the product.

There are many other ways to choose your independent surveyor and you should ensure that the surveyor is in fact genuinely fully independent. Some consider it appropriate to instruct the building society valuer to carry out the survey, at the same time. In such a case, the valuer has effectively two paymasters with very different requirements and you want to be sure that the choice of your surveyors is someone who will have only your interests in mind and be fully independent.

There are times when estate agents may encourage you to use "their own surveyors" who will be presented as an independent company although sometimes may form part of the same group of companies as the estate agent selling the property. You would need to decide, yourself, whether those working under the same umbrella group of companies are likely to offer the same level of genuine independence from each other or whether you feel this could amount to a conflict of interest.

Would you feel more secure in the knowledge you were instructing your own independent company of surveyors who have no links at all to any companies within the group of the selling agent?

The aim of the estate agent is to achieve a sale on a property at the highest price with minimal interruptions to that sale. Your independent surveyor's report is designed to give you a true picture of the condition of the property and any other relevant legal factors, warts and all, and will be your key tool in allowing you to negotiate the final purchase price at the correct level.

Once you have your surveyor's independent survey report to hand you should study the document thoroughly and read it through several times. It is also very important that your surveyors offer you a first class after sales service and as many one to one conversations with you, as you need, to explain any elements of concern you have in the report.

Your surveyor should allow time to explain those concerns which require clarification in order that you can then move on to negotiate your final offer price.

Negotiate the final offer price using your professional advisors.

It is quite probable that you have either never negotiated an offer price on property or you have only done it once or twice before in your life. Also, you may not be comfortable with negotiating, not everybody is. People can become embarrassed by asking to reduce a holding price by many thousands of pounds, even when it has been fully justified through the contents of your surveyor's independent survey report.

Negotiation is normally done now, by having a face-to-face conversation with the selling agent. The agent will be vastly more experienced in negotiating property prices than you are. A good estate agent will keep you purchasing at the highest possible price to serve their client, the seller of the property, and will potentially earn more commission by doing that.

You must protect your financial interests.

To negotiate your final offer price after your independent surveyors report has been received, it would be wise, if you prepare a separate email highlighting the key areas on which your final negotiated price will be based.

Under no circumstances should you release the full content of your confidential independent survey document to any of the parties acting for the other side of the transaction. You have paid a fee for that survey report. Its content is private and confidential and is to be used solely on your side of the transaction in order to negotiate the final purchase price. Your surveyor's independent survey report will typically contain a specific clause indicating that it is not to be released to third parties, other than your legal advisors, and it is important you adhere to this contractual requirement.

Maintaining the confidentiality of the survey report is a very important part of protecting against any possibility of misuse or misrepresentation by third parties.

A good way to describe the price at which property is marketed is to consider this as a provisional, marketing price. At the time the property is put on the market, there has been no professional, technical inspection of any kind. The suggested price at which it is marketed can only be based on its superficial condition and hence that is a provisional marketing price.

However, after you have received your surveyor's independent survey report, you will now know the true condition of the property. It is on the basis of the true condition that the final offer price should be made and the negotiation needs to take this into account. Prospective buyers will often want to know the cost of the various works required to be done in the property they are purchasing. In order to arrive at an accurate figure, you would need to obtain several independent contractor's reports, in order to consider the differences in the various prices which they are likely to quote.

If a property is clearly dated or in need of modernisation then it is realistic to assume the provisional marketing price which the estate agent has applied to the property would reflect the cost of some of these obvious works. Even a superficial inspection can tell you if the kitchen or bathroom is old and will need refitting, or if the decorations are from a different era and warrant modernisation.

Negotiation is not just about adding up the cost of everything that needs doing to bring the property up to a fully modern and safe standard. It is about uncovering the "hidden items" which only come to light after a professional, fully independent survey report.

Your surveyors can advise and guide you through the negotiation process by suggesting to you an appropriate range within which it would be appropriate to negotiate the purchase price. This range would be based on an accurate knowledge of the condition of the property which you will only be able to determine, after your surveyor's independent survey report has been forwarded to you.

In conclusion, these are the key points to follow when buying property...

> 1. Make sure you are given enough time to view the property to begin with.

> 2. Show your genuine interest to purchase by agreeing to pay the full asking price which will be subject to negotiation after your independent survey report.

> 3. Instruct your fully independent survey report at the earliest opportunity making sure your surveyor is not connected to any other parties involved in the transaction or working for anyone other than yourself.

4. Once you have received your survey report, do not share this with anybody other than your legal advisors.

5. Make sure you speak with your surveyor to get clarity on everything in the report and to establish a suitable negotiation price range to put forward to the selling agent and sellers for consideration.

6. Negotiate your final offer price by emailing the figure and the reasoning behind that figure, from the relevant content of your surveyor's independent survey report that the negotiation stance is based on.

By following these simple steps, it is likely you could save thousands of pounds. You will be investing safely in your new home, protecting yourself and your family in the knowledge that you have negotiated wisely and correctly on the basis of knowledge given to you through your surveyor's independent survey report.

Always remember, the only person on your side with the professional technical knowledge to look after your interests is your genuinely independently instructed surveyor. They have a specific legal and contractual duty of care to you as the buyer. The estate agent of course has a contractual arrangement with the seller of the property.

Whatever you need to know about the property or any explanation you require concerning the mortgage valuation or anything in your independent survey report, it is imperative you discuss these issues with your independent surveyor.

Your independent surveyor is there to help make your move the right move.

TIME TO WEEP

Nothing can cause upset between friends, families or couples quite like buying a property.

We all have very individual ideas of the features that most interest us when buying a new home and the likelihood of these coinciding exactly with those of your partner are not always the same. The exciting prospect of buying a new home can often exacerbate these differences. We can all become easily swayed by the obviously good features of a property and as a result, perhaps, have a tendency to overlook the negative aspects.

In such an emotionally fraught scenario it is easy to see how disagreements can occur. Surprisingly, this can even happen when you are buying a property on your own without any partner's wishes to consider. It is very tempting, even as a sole purchaser, to look at the lovely room sizes, all the beautiful views, and not give proper consideration to the negative factors, often until it is too late and you have already committed to or completed on the purchase.

Buying property is an expensive process and if you get even a small part of it wrong, this can become a very costly mistake and not only in monetary terms. Having to come to terms with problems in your newly acquired property that may not be easily remedied and that might have been foreseen, could impact on the initial happiness felt when first taking possession of your 'dream' home. Perhaps, even leaving you disillusioned at the situation you now find yourself in.

Judgement can become clouded when we look at houses and flats to buy and so you need an independent view of things to sometimes put you back on the right track. Friends and family will often offer their views as well your partner, if you are buying as a couple but inevitably it is part of human nature, when making a big decision, to think that we, as an individual, know best and to tend to push away the negative comments made by others.

This book is about providing you with a professional and detached view of elements of property which need to be carefully considered in terms of how they might impact on future serviceability, cost and, very importantly, the prospect of selling the property when that time eventually comes.

At yoursurveyors.com we have over 50 years of property expertise and during that time we have had literally thousands of conversations with buyers of property, and we are able to bring together all of that knowledge and experience to help you make an informed decision when considering purchasing a property.

You may choose not to listen to your partner, friends or family when making such a momentous and personal decision because of your proximity to them. The following examples are of situations we have seen and the views that others have taken or have come to, in usage, in the hope that this will be of benefit to you. The accompanying advice will allow you to consider calmly and dispassionately what would be the best course to take with the property you are thinking of buying.

Parking

One thing that really raises the temperature of homeowners is parking.

How we park, where we park, and how convenient and available the parking is, can be very important parts of the decision-making process which people sometimes don't give enough thought to when they are bowled over by the pretty little cottage with a lovely kitchen and bathroom and roses around the door. What we offer you here are some cold hard facts to consider whether, in very different circumstances from those you experienced when you first viewed the property, you will be as happy with the decision you then made, moving forwards.

In an ideal world, everybody would have off-street parking for however many cars they own and peace would reign. In practical terms the reality is different. None of us has an endless pot of money when buying property and so inevitably we accept some shortcomings in the properties we are able to select.

Parking often comes under this category. You may find a property that is eminently suitable, however, there is no off-street parking. It may well be that when you first view this property it is during a quiet time and you're able to easily park directly outside and walk straight into the property, so the lack of any off-street parking doesn't seem to be a problem.

What is important is that you revisit the property location during differing times before making a decision. It is often the case that when everybody is home from work or at the weekends you may need to park a long way away from the property, perhaps even in a different street. This has a number of implications.

Firstly, either owning or considering buying an electric car would be problematic, as you would be unable to plug in your car to charge it when you're 100 yards away. Consider coming back from the shops with three or four bags of heavy shopping and perhaps, children in the car as well and suddenly there is a downpour of rain. This is a very different picture from when you may have first viewed the property and were able to park outside in the street and walk straight in on a lovely sunny day.

Or imagine if you leave in a hurry and having walked 100 yards to your car, you suddenly remember you forgot your wallet, purse or credit card. In contrast, it may be that you are lucky enough to have a garage with your property. However, you should always measure this garage at its narrowest and shortest points as many garages built for properties in the 1930s and 50s are far too small to accommodate the much larger modern vehicles.

Alternatively, you might be lucky enough to have a forecourt to park on at the front of the property with access from a driveway shared with your adjoining neighbours. This can work very well if you have agreeable and considerate neighbours who don't block the driveway, periodically, without considering your needs. However, this is not always the case and could lead to antagonism with your closest neighbours which is neither desirable nor pleasant, especially over the long-term.

Another inconvenience is for friends and/or family coming to visit who will suffer the same inconvenience as yourself if there is no readily available nearby parking option.

Other factors to consider with parking are the possible impact on saleability and value, the fact that you may need to apply for permits with associated cost implications for nearby parking and other general parking restrictions where applicable.

Steps And Slopes

When viewing a property, it is plain to see whether or not there are steps up to the front door or perhaps, steps down to the front door or either of these at the back of the property.

There are several points to consider with either situation.

How would you feel about using steps every time you go into and out of the property? It is a good idea to try and do a rough calculation of how many times you go in and out of your property on an average day and you'll find it is surprisingly more than you think. Now multiply that by the number of steps at the property whether that be up to or down to the front door or out into the rear garden, which could well be at a higher or lower level than the property.

Now imagine yourself using that many step ups every single day. If you see that as part of your daily exercise workout you may see it as a positive. However, consider the situation where your rear garden is elevated above the back of the property with 10 steps up to this first level and another five or six up to the very top level. You may find it a good idea to have a little sundeck or a work-shed at the back corner of the garden right at the top.

Off you go to carry out some work in your shed then suddenly realise you've forgotten something, so it's down the steps and back up again. A short while later, you need to use the toilet, so it's down the stairs and back up again. Shortly afterwards, somebody rings your electronic doorbell prompting you, on your phone, to answer the front door and it's down the stairs and back up again. Very quickly you've had to go up and down over 100 steps. Try attempting that in one go and see how you feel afterwards!

Another point to consider in a property where there are steps up or down, or from the front or rear, is that this will have implications for higher than average levels of rainwater falling towards the property at some point. There will be a need for this to be properly disposed of. A front door which is below the level of the forward street is a potential point for rainwater to flood and cause damp in the property. This will need very careful consideration in terms of surface water disposal, and sadly this is often not dealt with well. As an intending buyer, if you move into such a property, you could be faced with an immediate expense to put this situation right.

Young or healthy purchasers will often have no problem with steps of this kind. However, if a family decide to have children, the possible hazards engendered using steps by young children could be quite serious. If the property is bought by a mature couple; ageing, injury or mobility issues can severely impact on their quality of life, if they have to negotiate steep steps.

Changing levels are sometimes dealt with by slopes rather than steps and these also need careful attention when considering your future enjoyment of the property. A sloping driveway can be hazardous by directing rainwater to discharge towards your garage or the property. In winter conditions, if there is a build-up of ice, in extreme cases, this can stop you parking on your own driveway.

If your rear garden is long but sloped, this can create a problem when trying to cut the grass which is a continuing maintenance requirement in most cases. Running a lawnmower even if electrically or diesel powered over a sloping garden doesn't seem like too much of an issue until you've done it for 50 times when it becomes more than just a chore, especially for anyone with mobility issues.

Another thing to consider with sloping plots is that often to make them more usable, you will need to create separate sections of level garden. In order to achieve this, you will need to have constructed retaining walls. The construction of retaining walls is not cheap, and if it isn't done properly and under the supervision of a qualified structural engineer with a suitable design for strength and weep hole provision for drainage, then there will be an ongoing risk of a build-up of hydrostatic pressure on the retaining face. Over time this will cause these walls to fail with significant replacement costs.

Slopes and steps also need safety barriers and handrails and if these are not present in the property you will be faced with the cost of providing them.

Busy Roads

The impact on future saleability of a busy road fronting is really self-evident, so no need for us to go into huge detail about the poor health effects of fumes from vehicles as well as noise pollution, particularly on children and the elderly.

There are of course considerable variations of busyness and a secondary road sometimes used as a cut through during rush-hour is very different from properties which faced directly onto a main road.

Whilst it is true there are discounts to be had on these properties compared to similar properties on quieter roads, making them appear to be a bargain, it is equally important to be aware that the same discounts will apply when you come to sell the property in the future.

Living in a house where you, perhaps, cannot sensibly open some of the windows during the hot summer months because of pollution and noise is something people often forget.

Shops And Schools

Perhaps more generally we should say availability of facilities.

This is an area over which there is often disagreement. On the one hand if you have no shops available close to the property there is the argument that you can always jump in the car and in a relatively short space of time have access to a supermarket where you can do your weekly shop quite happily. On the other hand, sometimes, you just need a single item that you've forgotten, or you fancy a snack, or you want a newspaper. All the kinds of things that a little local shop can provide, and from our experience when they're not available people soon come to miss the convenience.

Schools of course are another issue. When it comes to the time for secondary schools, parents often move to a particular location in order to be within the catchment area for a school which they believe will be beneficial for the child's education. Another factor to consider is the ease of travel to and from school.

When children reach the age where they want some independence, it's reassuring to make sure that they will have a safe and reasonable journey to school rather than being in a location where transport could be difficult. This is especially so when mum or dad's taxi isn't always an available option.

Being close to a school can sometimes be seen as a benefit. However, it is always prudent to visit the property you're intending to buy near the times when school starts or finishes. This will allow you to evaluate the levels of traffic flow and build-up and how it is managed and how this might impact on the safety of your children and the ease of travelling to and from.

Orientation And Gardens

Something which is not always taken into consideration by homebuyers when they look to buy a property is its orientation, not only in relation to the gardens but also when considering the effect of solar heat gain or the lack of it on rooms in the property.

North facing rooms can be quite dark and cold at certain times of the year and if it is a room in which you hope to spend a good deal of time, then this might impact on your decision whether or not to buy that property. It just takes a few seconds with the many apps available nowadays to establish the orientation of the property and the impact this may have.

A north facing conservatory might be preferable in the summer months than a south facing conservatory as these additions to a property, in particular, can be subject to extreme heat gain during the hot, summer days.

If you have a large garden then the orientation of it may be less important than if the garden is quite compact. Consider the example of a mid- terraced three storey townhouse with a very small north facing rear garden. In such a case that garden may barely see the sunlight to any degree. The enjoyment of your garden in the summer months can be much reduced by the absence of much in the way of sunlight, although, if you are someone who prefers to stay out of the sun, then this could be a positive benefit.

A large garden when purchasing property can seem an attractive proposition and if you are a keen gardener with plenty of time on your hands then that can certainly be the case. However, if you are someone who doesn't have a lot of time to devote to gardening then it can become, not only a chore, but an expense. It might be necessary, at additional expense, to employ someone to come and tend to your garden to avoid it becoming ramshackle and reducing the value of your property if or when the time comes to sell.

Usually, there needs to be a balance, as well, between the size of the property and the size of the garden. A very large property with a very small garden won't appeal to many people, similarly, although the price, when it is offered for sale, can seem attractive to you as a buyer, the discount which the small garden forces upon it, will apply just as much to you when you come to sell in the future.

Structural Issues

For the majority of people being told through your surveyor's independent survey report that the property has structural issues would be enough to deter your purchase. However, in some cases, it may be reported by your surveyors that there are no indications of any current structural issues with the property but there have been in the past and perhaps the property has been completely or partially underpinned.

What should you do in that situation? Certainly, there are things you need to know.

In the first instance, it will be important to confirm exactly what happened in the past and that all the correct processes necessary were followed. Your surveyor's independent survey report will give you full details about this. After this, it is important that you make initial enquiries to insurance companies to confirm whether it is appropriate to continue with the existing insurance policy on the property through the same insurer, either with you as a new client, or whether you can seek alternative quotations from different insurers.

Experience has shown that when a property has been underpinned the likelihood is that insurance premiums you pay to insure the building in the future will be higher than on a property which has not been underpinned. It is also likely that the companies prepared to offer you insurance will be more limited in number.

There is a pattern of perception when it comes to previously underpinned properties which in over 50 years of surveying experience, we have noted. It seems that there is a proportion of people who will be happy to purchase a previously underpinned property once their surveyor's independent survey report has confirmed there are no indications of any continuing movement, on the basis that they feel the property is stronger, now that it has been subject to the underpinning works. However, another proportion of people, will not under any circumstances entertain a property which has been underpinned and from experience the split on these matters appears to be roughly 50-50.

Therefore, it is important to note that owning a property which has been subject to earlier underpinning works is likely to offer you reduced insurance options, more expensive insurance options and more limited marketability options when the time comes to sell.

As with any property purchase it is imperative to obtain your surveyor's independent survey report prior to making a decision as to whether or not to proceed, as the picture is more complex and requires professional interpretation on your behalf when underpinning is part of the issue. Certainly, when people consider the prospect of structural issues, they often expect that this will relate to the foundations having failed and the need for underpinning or similar works.

In reality your surveyor's independent survey report may well highlight many other potential structural issues in the property sometimes arising from works carried out without proper regulatory compliance, or modifications made to enlarge openings or create more space in the loft, for example, which can have long-term consequences if they have not been dealt with properly.

The Cellar Room

Initially, it can be quite exciting and appealing when you realise that the property you are thinking of buying has a study, games room or an office in the cellar. With freshly painted walls, bright spotlights and floor coverings, a cellar can appear to have been transformed from a dank and dusty area into a fantastic, extra piece of useful accommodation within the property.

Sadly, this is very unlikely.

With over 50 years of surveying expertise we can safely say that almost without exception cellars are damp.

We have lost count of how many times we have been proudly advised by the vendor of the property how the cellar is lovely and dry. Generally, a thorough testing with the damp meter confirms that exactly the reverse is true. The problem with damp, despite suggestions to the contrary, is you cannot see it and you cannot smell it even though you can sometimes see and smell the impacts which damp creates.

However, damp cellars aren't necessarily a problem, but they can certainly become more of a problem. When people start to change the way they were constructed; by concealing the damp and by concealing the problems which may exist behind the boarded linings, they provide the conditions and create the potential for those problems to become much worse.

Most cellars occur in Victorian properties and attempting to provide a long-term effective solution to make the cellars serviceable is extremely difficult to achieve and even more difficult to remain effective over the long term.

Inspection of the cellar is an important part of your surveyor's independent survey inspection and the guidance they will offer you in respect to this part of the property will be invaluable. Inappropriate cellar conversions can be a breeding ground for dry rot, the most damaging timber fungus you will experience and the most expensive and difficult to eradicate which can cause issues for mortgageability and impact the value of the property.

The Latin name for the dry rot fungus is serpula lacrymans. Serpula meaning "little snake" and lacrymans meaning "making tears".

An inappropriate modification of a Victorian cellar can certainly "make tears" and become for you a "time to weep".

SECRETS AND LIES

W hat is the difference between a secret and a lie, and how critical are these things when it comes to buying property? Is misdirection or avoidance about facts relating to a property when you are selling it the same as lying?

Certainly, the consequences to the purchaser of the property can be.

There are situations where people selling property will misdirect facts or avoid answering questions to serve their own ends, but equally, people who buy and sell property are not qualified surveyors, and often there will be problems which they themselves are not even aware of until your surveyors independent survey report is carried out.

What is it built of?

A great question, and one which can have a major impact not only on whether or not the purchase of the property should proceed, but also the implications of the construction for maintenance and running costs.

Non-Traditional

Let's first consider concrete construction. Some types of concrete construction are accepted as mortgage security by most lenders, and many have stood the test of time for a number of years. Others however are at the other end of the spectrum.

In the early 1980s, a fire occurred inside an "Airey" house which caused extensive damage. Most of the internal wall materials had been destroyed leaving the PRC (precast reinforced concrete) structure exposed to reveal a number of worrying structural defects. Serious cracking was found in the structural PRC columns caused by inadequate protection of the embedded steel reinforcements and chemical changes to the surrounding concrete.

Further investigations by BRE (Building Research Establishment) showed that a number of other house types built during the postwar rush to build new homes, exhibited similar defects, that would most certainly lead to eventual structural failure.

In 1984 the Government introduced legislation to compensate owners who had bought affected houses from the public sector under right to buy schemes. It was deemed that the severe structural defects could not have been identified during surveys at time of purchase due to the nature of the properties.

The Housing Defects Legislation (now Part XVI of the Housing Act 1985) allowed the Secretary of State to designate particular dwelling types as inherently defective and empowered local authorities to operate a Scheme of Assistance for all eligible owners, either by way of buy back or by way of repair.

Over 28,000 households were aided under the Assistance Scheme, with only a small number of eligible properties not taking part.

Most 'repairs' were carried out using a system of repair which was licensed, inspected and certificated by PRC Homes Ltd, a subsidiary of NHBC, however not all owners chose this route.

Some local authorities carried out 'partial repairs' to their own stock, which unfortunately did not remove all the defective PRC structural elements from the dwellings. Unfortunately, this type of 'local repair' did not provide valid PRC certification, meaning that in many cases, the property remains unmortgageable to lenders.

PRC Homes LTD, closed down in 1996. Houses repaired under the licensed scheme were generally considered by some lenders to be acceptable for mortgage lending purposes with a standard NHBC warranty. The legislation did not allow for any improvement during repair, but superficially, the appearance of a reinstated houses changed dramatically, despite key identification characteristics such as window and door openings, and roof pitches, remaining constant.

It should again be stressed that the presence of a new brick skin alone on a defective house, does not in itself signify that the house has been repaired under an approved PRC repair scheme. PRC repair Certification is only issued to homes repaired under the PRC repair scheme and the certification document should always be viewed/ legally verified prior to sale or purchase.

In essence you could be buying a house which looks like it is of standard brick construction, but which has a chequered history and may not be a good purchase unless of course the proper procedures have been followed and the proper certification remains available.

Not all concrete houses however are problematic, and your surveyors independent survey report will advise you appropriately.

Timber Framed

There are in essence three main types of timber framed property to consider. Firstly, there are historic timber framed properties.

Timber-framed buildings are a striking feature in many of England's towns, villages, and farmsteads. Examples can date back to the 12th century, but most have 16th century origins. They continued to be built up to the 19th century in rural parts of the country. Often the timber-frame might be concealed by historic claddings, such as render, slate or tile-hanging and weatherboarding. Alternatively, the timber-frame can be fully exposed with infill panels of render, wattle and daub or brickwork. These buildings generally comprise large sections of hardwood timbers such as oak which by their type and size have exceptional durability which is why examples of these remain 500 years after they were built.

With more modern timber framed properties however, the situation is very different. These come under two categories which we might define as current timber framed properties and 1960s and 70s timber framed properties.

Current timber framed properties we might say have been around since the 1980s. There is a consistent and scientific methodology in the way that these properties are built. They have to be able to resist the damage which could occur if rainwater were allowed to penetrate into the property from outside, but equally must correctly use vapour barriers in their construction in order to allow breathability so that moisture inevitably produced by the occupants of the building can properly escape.

The mechanisms used to achieve this are well established and current timber framed properties can provide many years of serviceability and are generally widely accepted for mortgage security purposes.

The situation is quite different however in properties of timber framed construction built in the 1960s and 1970s or before. The well-established mechanisms used in current timber framed properties to protect the structural timber frame from rot were not as well established or adhered to in 1960s and 70s timber frame construction. Concerns previously raised about the longevity of these timber framed elements in a particular television exposé means that they are mostly not accepted for mortgage security purposes although they may be in some cases.

There are however a few special cases of timber framed properties built in the 60s and 70s which are accepted for mortgage purposes, but it is important that your surveyors independent survey report is able to identify these for you, and also to advise you further, where, as we have seen in some cases, modifications have been carried out which change a situation which was acceptable to one which no longer is.

"Not To My Knowledge"

If we had to guess, then we would imagine this is probably one of the most popular answers to solicitors' standard enquiries when the sellers of the property see that something might cause a problem.

Typical questions which might be asked could include, "have any walls or chimney breasts been removed at the property, has there ever been any party wall issues, have there been any instances of flooding, or are you aware of any problems with invasive plants?"

Problems with the answers to these questions could interrupt the progress of any sale and so a wary seller might choose when completing the solicitors' questionnaire to use the stock phrase "not to my knowledge".

It is easy of course when simply filling out a paper form in the comfort of your own home to choose this route. Very different however when you have an independent surveyor directly facing you, eye to eye and making a note not only of your answers but also gauging your physical responses to questions, something which as surveyors we inevitably gain experience of over the years.

The standard set of questions which your surveyors will ask the vendors is sometimes every bit as important a part of the process as the inspection itself. Albeit grudgingly, people tend to give honest answers when confronted directly with a verbal question. It's amazing how many things come to light only after your surveyor's independent survey report and such questioning.

We have had more than one occasion where even something as important as previous structural monitoring or even underpinning has never been disclosed to the purchasers until such time as the surveyor directly asked the question. It would be harsh to always describe the situation as being one where lies are being used but certainly there are times where elements of misdirection are apparent and it is your surveyor's independent inspection, questioning and report which reveals the secrets.

The Secret Areas

When we buy property, we all think that we have made a decent enough inspection to allow us to make the decision as to whether or not to spend hundreds of thousands of pounds and commit to a new home which we hope will be ours for many years to come. The truth is however that most people when inspecting a property to buy are certainly never given enough time to be able to make that decision, and also don't have the knowledge to be able to fully understand the financial commitment they are making.

Houses and flats are very complicated. They have usually been there for many years, in some cases hundreds of years, with different owners who often will have changed, modified, extended and manipulated them in all kinds of ways. These modifications are sometimes done professionally and very well with all necessary regulatory compliance. Often also however, they are not done professionally or well, and do not comply with the regulations necessary, either due to peoples ignorance of that fact or an attitude of "no one will see this so I don't care", or the classic "that doesn't need planning permission".

What many people fail to realise is that just because something doesn't need planning permission it frequently must comply with building regulations. Failure to understand the requirements for regulatory compliance is one of the secret areas of property missed by virtually every intending purchaser and only picked up during your surveyor's independent survey report.

The consequences of failing to comply with building regulations when removing walls, chimney breasts and the like could be catastrophic, as the failure to obtain independent confirmation of the adequacy of necessary support could lead to structural failure and collapse.

It is important to understand the role of building control.

With all building work the owner and occupier of the property or land in question is ultimately responsible for complying with the relevant planning rules and building regulations. The role of checking that building regulations are as far as can reasonably be determined being complied with, falls to a building control body.

It is not the role of building control to provide quality control of the works, to monitor every stage of the construction process, to provide a service to address issues such as the finish and aesthetics of the works, to provide a service to offer contractual protection between the person carrying out the work and the parties engaged in the design and/or construction of the work, nor to provide a guarantee of compliance with the building regulations.

It is important to note also that indemnity warranties offered where regulatory compliance has not been obtained in respect to such matters is often of no value whatsoever and is covered elsewhere in this book.

Other "secret areas" are considered so because the average intending purchaser when viewing the property simply doesn't look at them. This could include difficult to access side pathways, roof spaces, cellars, and in some cases even rooms congested or for whatever reason advised unavailable for inspection during the viewing.

We had a case where when the possible purchaser was viewing

the property, they were unable to inspect the garage because the seller advised that "the keys weren't around". As the inspecting surveyors of course, we insisted that we had to inspect this garage and in fact the keys were suddenly magically available, and inspection of the garage indicated very severe deficiencies to the point where there were stalactites hanging down from the concrete roof and the whole garage required demolition and full replacement at significant cost. Both a secret and a lie in that particular case.

Your surveyors are also quite adept at seeing what's around the property which the average intending buyer often misses, focusing as they do on the lovely kitchen and bathroom and the beautifully manicured gardens.

As surveyors we don't miss the fact that on the other side of the hedge there is a railway in a cutting, or nearby there is a pig farm, (yes we have seen that) or next door is a missed scrapyard (yes we have seen that) or even next door, that constant stream of gentlemen in and out indicates that upon further inquiry, next door there is a brothel (yes we have seen that too!).

Your surveyors independent survey report is about a lot more than just subsidence and damp. It is also about discovering the secrets and sometimes revealing the lies in whichever form those matters arise.

HOME IMPROVEMENTS OR REDUCING THE VALUE?

We Brits love to improve our homes; or do we?

Home improvements, whether major or minor, would appear to be a national obsession with the British public. We love to improve our properties, to enlarge them and make them more attractive, in all manner of ways.

Whether they are enthusiastic DIY projects, professional extensions or modifications, individual statements of design or following current fashions and trends, we Brits love to modify and 'improve' our home environment. However, the type and quality of the improvements one makes may not necessarily add to the value of your home and might detract from it. The alterations may even make it less attractive to a prospective buyer in the event that you wish to sell the property.

Therefore, when it comes to buying a property, it's important that you consider what has happened to that property over the years and whether you view those changes in a positive way. Are they likely to persuade you to consider making an offer for the property or even paying a little more to secure it? Would these elements need more careful professional assessment through your surveyor's independent inspection? Your surveyors will have seen hundreds of differing types of extension and property modifications over the years and are highly experienced in assessing their impact, whether positive or negative on the future value of the property.

All these assessments will be contained in your surveyor's independent report allowing you to make a decision with confidence.

Extensions

Financial considerations tend to dictate the type of property that we initially purchase. However, as time passes our circumstances change and there comes a point when we may decide that we need more space.

The most popular modification made to properties is an extension. It may be an extra reception room, enlarged kitchen or an extra bedroom for an addition to the family. The classic chalet style house has a long catslide roof and often, one of the bedrooms on the ground floor. It is a popular choice for many people in that you can add accommodation above the side elements of the property without taking up any of the surrounding land. Typically, extensions are added to the side or rear of the property, in which case, they will take up some of the available garden land.

Although the addition of an extension can increase the value of a property, if it takes up a disproportionate amount of the remaining land area, it can negatively impact on the value which adding the accommodation to the property has provided. It is important that a property has balance about it and taking away too much of the amenity land simply to add accommodation will often make a property less attractive to intending purchasers.

On one occasion, we surveyed a modest, terraced property that had been increased in size by adding a rear, single level extension. This reduced the size of the rear garden, and the situation was aggravated even more by the owner's decision to build a swimming pool in the remaining area of the garden. This effectively occupied all of the garden area, apart from a small pathway to walk around. To make matters worse, within close proximity to the rear of the property, was a twenty-storey block of local authority flats which directly overlooked the property and it's brand-new swimming pool. Now, we are not disputing that there would be some prospective buyers who might be happy with this arrangement, however, most, would definitely be deterred.

When buying property, it is easy to become emotionally attached to one single element rather than look at the bigger picture. Your surveyor is able to assess, dispassionately, on the basis of many years of experience evaluating such problems, what concerns are uppermost for most people and what they do and do not enjoy in property purchase.

Your surveyors role is not as straightforward as merely pointing out defects. A conscientious surveyor should support the client in making the right decision about subjective elements of property purchase. It is easy for you to fall in love with a property and not actually see it warts and all. Your surveyors are invaluable in helping you to arrive at an objective assessment.

When buying a property with an extension to the rear, it is necessary to consider how much that may impact on available, natural light in adjoining areas of the property. There was a fashion, in the fairly recent past, to construct these extensions without the benefit of any skylights or borrowed light coming in from the roof of the new extension itself. This can create a black hole in the areas which are being extended which is easily missed when viewing a property with all the lights on, at the time of inspection. Due to restricted viewing times prospective buyers are allowed by many estate agents to inspect a property, such problems are accentuated.

As the majority of people only move two or three times in their lives, it is unfair to expect them to have experience in knowing what to look out for. In the limited time allocated for a viewing, it is easy to overlook the faults in a property; especially, if it is being showcased in the best possible light.

Your surveyor's independent survey report will be able to advise you on the quality of any extensions.

A well-constructed, professionally built extension can certainly enhance a property but there are many things which can go wrong. We have seen many extensions constructed of inadequate materials, such as shallow timber framed sections, or single skin, or half brick. Even in extensions properly constructed, with an appropriate thickness of brick and block and adequate insulation, this does not guarantee the quality of the finished article.

Keen DIY enthusiasts will sometimes try to construct an extension themselves. However, such attempts are rarely without faults and although some are good, they are often, terrible.

We inspected a property where there had been a need to replace brickwork along the main left wall of the property. The owner had decided to take on the task themselves and proudly confirmed to the surveyor not only that they had done this, but that before they did it they had never ever laid a brick before. It is difficult to fully describe the state of the brickwork, but if you can imagine that a properly constructed brick wall should be effectively smooth and flush between each brick, the contrast here was quite staggering. The unevenness of the jointing from brick to brick created a series of tiny projecting brick shelves on which' mini ornaments could easily have been placed. Perhaps an interesting look for a modern art installation but in this case, a terrible trap for moisture to encourage dampness into the building. Your surveyor's detailed inspection report would have been the only way this would have been picked up. The brickwork, in question, was down a very congested side area of the property. It is highly unlikely an intending purchaser would have ventured there.

Enthusiasm is rarely an adequate substitute for professional

expertise.

Loft Conversions

The attraction of a loft conversion is the fact that none of the amenity land or garden around the property will be taken away, by providing extra accommodation in the roof space. With some exceptions, there is often no need to obtain planning permission for loft conversions as they frequently fall within permitted development rights. However, what many people fail to realise is that, even though you don't need planning permission, you certainly do need building regulations permission in order to confirm the structural adequacy of what you are doing. Even if the loft modifications have not been designed in order to create habitable accommodation but merely to create central storage to the loft, there are concerns which are frequently raised in your surveyor's independent survey report.

You would also need to confirm that, when you are adding an additional storey height to the building, there is proper compliance with the requirements for means of escape, in the event of fire and associated matters. What initially appears to be a useful extra room or helpful storage in a boarded loft, may result in unforeseen and therefore unbudgeted financial costs in order to rectify structural or safety deficiencies.

Internal Upgrades

As surveyors, we never cease to be amazed with the number and variety of all manner of "improvements" we have seen over the years that people have made to their properties.

As has been previously mentioned, possibly because of a rushed viewing and a lack of knowledge, the intending buyers either haven't realised the implications of these "improvements" or have seen them but not understood the cost implications in order to remove, modify or simply replace elements which future prospective buyers might not consider favourably.

It is the fully independent and practical eye which the surveyor casts over the property that can sometimes bring you back to the reality of the situation from the "rose tinted glasses view" formed when hunting for a new home.

Let us have a look at a few examples...

The Study/Gym/Games Room In The Cellar

Whatever name you care to use, all of the above, usually, amount to much the same thing.

Upgrading cellars is difficult. Cellars are below the surrounding ground which means that the walls which form the cellar will be subject to hydrostatic pressure. This is where the pressure of water in the surrounding ground pushes against the wall and over time, will appear on the other side of the wall, within the cellar itself.

There are ways in which cellars can be converted and turned into serviceable spaces. In the vast majority of cases, however, attempts which are made to convert cellars into habitable spaces are ineffective and they become simply internally boarded areas concealing a multitude of potential future problems such as damp, rot and decay.

The first thing to enquire about if you are viewing a property which purports to have a usable cellar is to find out who undertook the works in order to confirm that they were undertaken by a company experienced in upgrading cellar accommodation. It is also important to confirm that the works are fully indemnified against any defect and rectification costs in the future. This should, in turn, be underwritten by a long-term insurance backed guarantee which your legal advisors should then confirm will remain effective even if the company which carried out the work should cease trading. It would also be important to confirm that liability in respect of the works, devolved exclusively to one single company, with no confusion over liabilities if more than one contractor or company was involved in the works.

The Million Pound Kitchen

We confess to some deliberate exaggeration here, in order to make a point. The point is that you will sometimes be tempted or even encouraged into paying too much money for a property which has been over capitalised.

The classic example would be where somebody has spent an excessive amount of money on a kitchen or bathrooms, over and above what the property warrants.
There are people who believe that if you spend £50,000 on a kitchen that it will add £50,000 to the value of the property. This is patently untrue, and we have seen many examples to confirm this.

Spending excessive amounts of money on a property which is in itself of modest size and accommodation will not reap financial benefits. A modern, well fitted kitchen and bathrooms most certainly do increase the value of the property but adding excessive cost and fanciful gadgetry has been shown, over the years, not to provide a return consistent with the cost of the installations.

If you are buying property, don't be tempted to pay too much for one which has been overcapitalised in this way. Conversely, if you are modernising or improving your property with a view to selling it at some point in the relatively near future beware of overspending.

The Beautiful Failure

Things which catch the eye of a buyer, often recently introduced to enhance saleability, will often be viewed in a much more pragmatic way through your surveyor's expert eyes in preparing their independent survey report.

That beautifully paved driveway or rear terrace so recently built and gleaming, while still new, can seem a wonderful feature in the property, but has it been provided with proper drainage? How are the slopes around the property? Will they encourage rainwater to flood towards the property causing the walls to become damp? Are they at the correct levels; or have they been laid in such a way that they "bridge" the damp proof course, creating a further risk of dampness over time, to the property?

On a recent property we surveyed, a property owner had spent tens of thousands of pounds providing beautifully rendered and white painted walls to achieve different levels within the raised, terraced, rear garden. However, what they had failed to do was to ensure that the walls were constructed and specifically designed so as to accommodate the forces which would be applied upon them. This would have allowed the discharge of rainwater through them, by the use of weepholes, an imperative in retaining structures. Without a correct statement of facts provided to our clients in your surveyor's independent survey report, they could easily have moved in and soon been faced with structural collapse of the retaining walls leading to expenditure running into many thousands.

Our report also averted the danger which the threat of collapsing walls might bring to anybody in the garden at the time, especially young children. There are a myriad of things which as surveyors we see and highlight in our reports. These can and often do, have a significant impact on the purchasing decision. It may highlight the need to reconsider the value of the original offer price made against the property once the knowledge of the actual condition of the property is made available to the buyer.

Always remember, the true cost of buying a property which is:

Purchase cost plus repair cost plus ongoing maintenance and running cost.

THE ENERGY PUZZLE

Nowadays, more than ever energy is a hot topic when it comes to buying property. Making your home as energy efficient as possible has a greater impact on your monthly outgoings now than ever before and a well-insulated energy efficient property also throws good light on your eco-credentials as we all face the continuing and increasing problems of climate change.

Energy in homes is a critical aspect of modern living as it powers various appliances, provides heating and cooling, and contributes to overall comfort and convenience. However, the consumption of energy in homes also has significant environmental and financial implications. Therefore, it is essential to understand and implement energy-efficient practices to reduce energy consumption and promote sustainability.

As originally constructed, it is mostly true to say that the older the property you are buying the less thermally efficient it is likely to be before improvements and uprating is carried out.

Victorian housing stock of which there are vast amounts throughout the UK was originally constructed mostly with 9-inch solid brick walls, ventilated timber ground and first floors and pitched roofs with no insulation in the roof space, all supplemented by timber single glazed windows.

This is almost as thermally inefficient as you can possibly get. However, the good news is that all properties of whatever kind can be made more thermally effective, and costs need not always be high.

If we take the example of the Victorian house, there are several measures that could be applied.

The modern tendency is to replace single glazed windows with double or even triple glazing often with UPVC or thermal break aluminium frame surrounds. This is a good start not only because the double-glazed units improve thermal efficiency compared to single glazing but the draught sealing around the windows further helps to reduce heat loss from the property compared with draughty old timber single glazed units.

There will be situations however with certain listed buildings and conservation area restrictions where you may not be able to carry out such work. In such cases the possibility of applying internal secondary glazing although less beneficial can also have some positive impact.

Another area where benefits of reducing heat loss can be quickly achieved is in the loft. Even after many years it is not uncommon to see lofts in Victorian houses with little or even no insulation material between the ceiling joists of the rooms below at all. Installing a good thickness of insulation quilt is a very effective way of retaining heat within the property and reducing fuel costs.

It is important though to ensure that the insulation is not tightly tucked into the eaves as this can restrict ventilation leading to condensation occurring within the roof space. If left unnoticed, condensation over time could start to drip onto the insulation below, not only reducing the effectiveness of the insulation material but eventually damaging the ceilings in the rooms which sit underneath the roof space.

Installing such insulation is usually within the capabilities of most homeowners and therefore need not be an expensive undertaking but can show immediate benefits to the property.

Where a property has a suspended timber ground floor, it is

possible in various ways to install insulation underneath the floorboards if suitable support is provided to the insulation itself and that care is taken to maintain adequate ventilation to the subfloor timbers, without which the possibility of potential decay could be created.

The most common form of heating we see during our inspections is the typical gas boiler with radiators although of course many other systems exist. Upgrading a dated boiler and even dated and relatively inefficient radiators will certainly provide a more effective solution to the heating requirements of the building. This when coupled with introducing individual thermostatic radiator valves or zonal controls is another effective way of improving the efficiency of the building and reducing fuel costs.

Depending on circumstances and locations other options to consider are air source or ground source heat pumps, heat recovery systems, biomass boilers and a myriad of other options which in various ways can improve efficiency compared to a classically outdated old-fashioned either centralised control heating system or individual unit heaters without central or remote controls at all.

Renewable energy sources such as solar panels or wind turbines are becoming increasingly popular in homes. These systems harness clean and sustainable energy from the sun or wind, reducing reliance on traditional energy sources and lowering carbon emissions. Installing solar panels on rooftops can generate electricity or heat water for household use, while wind turbines can be suitable for homes in windy areas. In some cases, excess energy generated can be fed back into the grid, further reducing energy costs.

A further option to consider when increasing the levels of insulation in a dwelling is the application of insulation material such as insulating board or render which depending on the material utilised can be applied either externally or internally.

External application will of course likely impact on the appearance of the building and again if the property is situated in a conservation area or is listed there well may be no option to do this. Installing insulation board or similar internally can be an option but will of course to some extent reduce the size of the accommodation within the property. Installing insulation requires very careful detailing around fixtures, fittings, window and door reveals, adjacent to skirtings and the like to achieve a satisfactory result.

Where a property is of brick and block cavity wall construction, there is often the possibility to inject insulation within the wall cavities if there is none present. This is a relatively straightforward and inexpensive proposition and can show immediate returns in respect of reducing heating costs and increasing comfort within the building.

Lighting is another area where energy consumption can be reduced. Traditional incandescent light bulbs are highly inefficient and consume more energy than newer alternatives. Switching to energy-efficient LED or CFL bulbs can significantly reduce energy usage and lower electricity bills. Additionally, utilizing natural light through well-placed windows and skylights can minimize the need for artificial lighting during the day.

Energy efficiency within a home has become an important factor to people when buying property. Your surveyors report will assess the current Energy Performance Certificate and will identify any inaccuracies or discrepencies. Depending on the level of survey chosen, the report may also include advice on how to improve the rating.

INSURE, ARE YOU SURE?

Insurance cover is ubiquitous in all areas of modern life. Insurance gives us a feeling of comfort. We insure so many things, health, mobile phones, cars and of course our properties and their contents.

The very fact that we take out an insurance policy makes us feel that we are fully protected and have done the prudent thing. We feel that whatever misfortune occurs we won't suffer because we have our insurance.

Indemnity Insurance

When it comes to buying property, there is one particular insurance which your solicitors may offer you which is something you may not have come across before. Indemnity insurance is a protection policy sometimes purchased during housing transactions. For a one-off payment the indemnity insurance policy protects you from a specific potential problem with a property that could cost you in the future if the requirement to repair or replace is forced upon you by a third party. For example, if you are buying a property and the seller can't provide a building regulation certificate then your conveyancing solicitor might suggest taking out an indemnity policy to cover potential costs. This will only cover any costs in the future if your local authority pursues a claim because you don't have the certificate. It's important to note that this insurance does not cover the cost of repairing defective items in your property.

For example, there might be a risk of a potential structurally inadequate element of the property such as an unsupported chimney breast, an inadequate roof frame, or insubstantial supporting beam to a removed wall. The risks of these elements catastrophically failing are not in any way covered by the indemnity insurances which you are likely to be offered.

The key wording in these policies is to be carefully noted:
'The policy will cover loss of market value, damages and expenses arising in complying with any enforcement notice/proceedings served by the appropriate authority.'

In practice this type of retrospective enforcement is extremely rare.

Unless the narrow limitations of indemnity insurance cover are clearly explained to a potential buyer, they may be under the mistaken belief that their indemnity insurance fully protects them for possible future repairs or replacement. In these circumstances you could end up with a huge bill and no insurance cover whatsoever.

For example, if there was an indemnity policy in place because you didn't have the installation certificate for a boiler it wouldn't cover repair or replacement of the boiler. For this reason, it is always important when you are considering purchasing a property to obtain a fully independent survey report from your surveyors. If recommended within that you should also have the service installations checked by a competent contractor.

New Build Insurance

New build warranties are issued to protect buyers from the costs of fixing structural defects caused by faulty materials or poor workmanship during construction. What they normally don't cover is damage from general wear and tear over time or damage caused by weather and natural events.

A standard new build warranty covers the finished property for 10 years from the date of completion including an initial 2-year defects insurance period, followed by an 8-year period for the remainder. Fixtures and fittings are usually only covered during those first two years. These warranties are property specific so should transfer over to any subsequent owners in the relevant period. Confirmation of transfer of the warranty to you as the new owner is something your legal advisors must do on your behalf.

It would be very unwise to buy any property under 10 years old without a suitable warranty. Originally, these warranties were pretty much exclusively offered by the NHBC (National House Building Council) but nowadays there is more competition.

Therefore, it is very important to establish that any warranty offered will be one broadly accepted by mortgage lenders. If that isn't the case, you could face problems when you come to sell the property. A prospective buyer may be unable to secure a mortgage against it particularly in the ten-year period and consequently be unable to proceed.

A Professional Consultants Certificate, something previously known as an architect's certificate or CML certificate (Council of Mortgage Lenders), is issued by a chartered architect or surveyor on a newly built or converted property and is usually of a 6-year duration. Though it has been renamed and is officially called 'the Professional Consultants Certificate'.

This is an important document for a number of reasons but particularly if you or your purchaser want to take out a mortgage on a newly built property. Mortgage lenders will generally only lend money against a newly built property if it is protected by a warranty scheme such as NHBC warranty or in some cases a Professional Consultant's Certificate. Smaller builders and self-builders sometimes favour a Professional Consultant's Certificate because they are often as much as 50% cheaper than NHBC warranties. A Professional Consultants Certificate is only a warranty in the sense that the issuing professional undertakes (by means of a signed CML certificate) that the subject property has been built, extended, or altered in accordance with the approved plans, complies with building regulations and is to a good standard. This undertaking is primarily for the use of banks and building societies as security for a loan. The lender is provided with an assurance of the standard of construction which is backed by the issuing architect's or other professional's indemnity insurance.

Professional Consultants Certificates are issued as standard for six years cover which the council of mortgage lenders have approved for use in their standard format. You can also buy additional cover to give ten years protection.

Contractors Insurance And Guarantees

Much is made of work carried out on property by varying contractors and offered on completion with a guarantee.

There is an old joke about somebody buying a second-hand car and being told it comes with a guarantee. "3 years or until you leave the showroom whichever comes first". Over the years this is similar to the situation which has prevailed with building works in general.

Most building contractors have no formal qualifications at all. Therefore, it is very difficult to assess the likely quality of the work they will produce or its practical value during its usage over time. The reality is that any guarantees offered are normally verbal and consequently have no substance. Sometimes a guarantee will be put forward which at first glance may seem useful but on closer inspection will often be seen to be nothing more than a materials guarantee. The materials which are being used have been subject to appropriate regulation and process in production and development but any inadequacy of application by generally unqualified contractors will leave you with no recourse of any kind.

Sadly, it remains the case that with general building works you are unlikely to be able to obtain any form of valid long-term insurance backed guarantee. However, with particular individual elements, there are options available to you.

Let's look at roofing, and advice given online by the NFRC (National Federation of Roofing Contractors):

> 1. Select up to three roofing contractors to look at the job. If possible, obtain recommendations from family, friends, neighbours, or a reputable trade association.

> 2. Ask each of them to give advice on which materials they would suggest using.

> 3. Invite quotes from each contractor but do not automatically take the cheapest option. Base your choice on the quality of the advice given and your confidence in the contractor.

> 4. Ask for a guarantee on new or refurbishment work. NFRC recommend purchasing an Insurance Backed Guarantee (IBG) which backs up, but is independent of, the contractor's own guarantee. Remember that even the best contractors can go out of business whereupon their own guarantees become worthless so make sure you will be covered.

> 5. Bear in mind that 'estimates' for refurbishment work can change once the chosen contractor has removed the main covering (e.g. tiles/slates) to expose the sub-structure underneath.

> 6. Agree payment terms before the work commences. Be careful on upfront payments. Ensure you know what you are getting for any upfront payment. It may be difficult to

get monies back. Contractors offering cash/VAT-free deals are not easily tracked down if things go wrong.

A further example of remedial work that may be required on the property you intend to purchase is that of dampness. Dampness whether rising, or penetrating, or both, can have serious long-term consequences and provide ideal conditions for the spread of associated timber infestation (woodworm) and decay. Gradually over many years this particular area of property maintenance and improvement has become more regulated, and the use of insurance backed guarantees from reputable companies are now commonplace.

The primary professional body for contractors working in this field is the Property Care Association (PCA) and you should look for any companies quoting for works to be a member of this body. The PCA offer this information and guidance on their website.

1. Members are required to have comprehensive industry recognised qualifications.

2. They are regularly audited to ensure the high standards of the Association are maintained.

3. They are able to offer insurance backed guarantees, required to adhere to a formal code of conduct and ethics and to adhere to minimum performance standards.

4. Expected to co-operate with the PCA in the unlikely event of any problems or complaints.

5. Licensed under the Government's TrustMark scheme (contractor members)

6. Able to access a deposit protection scheme for damp proofing, timber preservation, structural waterproofing and structural repair works.

In general terms therefore it is important to enquire through your legal advisors and what works if any have been undertaken previously. Ideally, they should be the subject of guarantees which are covered by an independent insurance policy. It is also important for your legal advisors to verify that the benefit of such guarantees will be fully transferable to you as the new owner of the property even though the original instruction for the works may have come through a third party.

Insuring Your New Home

As most people are aware you must insure your new home against all the usual risks of fire, flood, storm, and subsidence damage. A typical standard buildings insurance policy will offer a perfectly adequate cover for all the above.

Your legal advisors will inform you that it is imperative that you should insure your new property not from the date that you move in but from the date that you exchange contracts. At that point you are legally committed to moving ahead with the purchase and could face penalties if you fail to do so. A situation which is often not considered by a prospective buyer but which we at yoursurveyors.com have knowledge and experience of adds another twist to the need to insure your new property correctly.

Subsidence in property can be a problem that can only be remedied at great expense to the owner. It is extremely important that there is no uncertainty over whether you have insured your property adequately for this. If subsidence does occur, it is equally important that your policy states clearly the responsibility of the insurers to adequately finance the cost of the expensive repairs.

A situation we were linked to, developed many years ago in which a property was inspected and professionally surveyed and correctly advised as not having any issues of structural movement or subsidence. The client moved into the property but within a few short months severe cracks opened. There had been no signs of any risk of this at the time the survey was carried out, so the surveyor's report was correct in all regards.

Unfortunately, the purchasers of the property had taken out buildings insurance on it with a different insurer from the one that had previously been used by the previous owners. The cracks had appeared so quickly and were of such severity that the new insurers were claiming that these defects must certainly have been there before they took on the new insurance on the property. They argued that the movement must have started before they took on the risk of insuring the property and they were not liable and in consequence they were not contractually liable to pay for the expensive subsidence repairs.

In situations such as this there is a need to prove the condition of the property before the new insurers took on the risk.

At yoursurveyors.com we generally retain on file several hundred photographs of each property we survey which can then be relied upon to confirm the condition of the property before the new insurers take the risk on. The photographs used in such circumstances would indeed prove our client's case and make certain they were not left without insurance and a large bill for repairs.

Your surveyors independent survey report continues to serve your needs as a client sometimes long after you have moved into the property.

FIRE, FLOOD AND THEFT

Your home can be at risk from forces of nature with climate change playing its part or human error which can also put your property in danger. Here, we bring to your attention situations to take care with.

Fire

The annual statistics surrounding house fires in the UK are shocking and often tragic and all homeowners ought to be made aware of the dangers as a matter of course. However, this is often not the case. On average, 42 people die each year because their smoke alarm is not working. Most fires start when people are cooking. Every 6 days someone dies in a home fire started by a cigarette. Faulty electrics cause around 4,000 fires in the home each year.

There are four fundamental fire safety principles for preventing fire events and managing their impact:

1. Prevention

2. Detection and Communication

3. Occupant Protection

4. Containment and Extinguishment

Your surveyor's independent survey report will be of huge benefit in pointing out key elements in the property relating to fire prevention safety and means of escape. A typical example of an increased fire risk is when a property which was originally built over 2 levels is modified usually by the addition of a loft conversion, enabling accommodation over 3 and sometimes 4 levels.

With accommodation over three or more floors, it is prudent in our opinion to have fire resisting self-closing doors throughout the property and mains wired smoke detectors on yearly service contracts. Windows permitting exit for escape are required at all levels above ground floor. Where staircases are not separated from accommodation this also worsens the position for means of escape.

The regulations, as they currently stand at the time of going to print no longer require that the fire resisting doors which you should provide when forming an upper floor loft conversion need to be self-closing. At yoursurveyors.com we find this disturbing as what is the point of having a fire resisting door which does not close?

As the above example clearly shows an independent survey report from your surveyor affords you peace of mind and security.

When considering a possible, future property it is always necessary to obtain a detailed report from a qualified electrical contractor about the condition of the electrical installation. As previously stated, faulty electrics cause about 4,000 fires in the home each year. Nevertheless, before you go to this extra expense your surveyor's report will be able to provide you with a number of very pertinent insights relating to the installation. Concerns we frequently see include plastic fuse boards, dated or broken fittings, inadequate numbers of sockets, inappropriate switching and unsafe skirting mounted sockets. They are all indicators of a need for upgrading and modernisation to reduce the fire risk associated with substandard electrical installations.

Your surveyor will thoroughly inspect the roof space as part of the independent survey report and will check for adequate fire separation between dwellings. If any inadequacies are found this could invalidate your buildings insurance in the event that you need to make a claim. This could also impact on any future sale, as a prospective buyer would be unable to obtain a mortgage if they could not obtain buildings insurance.

Your surveyor's independent survey report will give you professional advice which follows common sense and good practice, often going beyond the minimum regulatory requirements, to provide you with information tailored to the specific issues relating to the property in question.

Flood

One of the questions your independent surveyor will typically ask the vendor when undertaking your survey is whether during their period of occupation the property has been subject to flooding at any time.

It is surprising how frequently the answer to that question is yes. This often happens when at some point during the previous owner's occupation, water has escaped from pipes in the property and consequently caused damage, sometimes leaving a trail of stains yet to be remedied. The surveyor will use a damp meter to check whether there is a risk of the problem not having been properly remedied or whether the stains are dry and indicate an old situation.

Uncontained or penetrating water and buildings are always a bad mix. Building components are not designed to deal with being made wet, whether that is through leakages in pipes internally or through dampness penetrating through the building external fabric, which is specifically designed to resist this. Leaking water has the potential to cause electrical shorts and in turn the risk of fire damage. If there are timbers which come into contact with excess water, there is the risk of decay. When the damp conditions come together in a particular way, this decay can come in the form of dry rot.

Dry rot is a very disruptive and expensive problem, difficult to remove and repair in properties. A differentiation is made between dry rot and other forms of fungal decay such as wet rot which although still serious is less concerning than dry rot which can spread unnoticed and affect timber a long way from the original source of the problem. In a situation some years ago, dry rot which started in a cellar spread unnoticed behind plaster right the way through the house from bottom to top. The dry rot eventually destroyed timbers not only in the cellar and ground floor but throughout the property to the first floor and roof timbers. The bill for replacement ran into thousands of pounds.

Often, it is the unnoticed pipe leak which carries on for a long time which can create the most disturbance. An example of this is when water pipes are carried beneath a suspended timber floor and can have slight leakages, in some cases for years. When the floorboards are lifted the whole of the floor void is found to be flooded. This can cause significant issues of condensation within the property whilst the owners are unaware that there is a 'swimming pool' underneath their feet the whole time. If at the same time, there is inadequate through ventilation for such a timber floor this creates the perfect conditions to encourage dry rot.

Your surveyor can assess situations where the required ventilation for timber floors has been completely blocked often for an extended period by the construction of conservatories, extensions, raised rear paving, or the provision of the ubiquitous timber decking.

Other forms of flooding can occur from natural disasters such as rivers overflowing and coastal surges from the sea. Pluvial (rainfall) flooding can be exacerbated by inadequate consideration of surrounding external surfaces to a property and the need for these to discharge water away from the building and not towards it.

Where your property is situated below the level of the forward road this increases the risk of flooding to the property during storm conditions unless proper consideration has been given to the need to collect and dispose of rainwater during these times. Additionally, a steeply sloping drive or access path can be a winter hazard. No one wants to find themselves unable to drive away from their property in a sudden emergency because overnight snow or a drop in temperatures has made it impossible to get their car off the icy drive.

Flooding poses a significant risk to people, communities, and the built environment with approximately 1.9 million people across the UK currently living in areas at significant risk from either river, coastal or surface water flooding. The number of people at risk could double as early as the 2050s. River and surface flooding already pose a severe risk to UK infrastructure with each flooding episode adding new evidence to underpin the significant magnitude of the threat. Currently all infrastructure services are at a greater exposure to surface water flooding than river flooding.

The latest State of the UK Climate Report indicates the UK has become wetter over the last few decades, although with significant annual variation. 2011-2020 was 9% wetter than 1961-1990. From the start of the observational record in 1862, six of the ten wettest years across the UK have occurred since 1998. The number of days where rainfall totals exceed 95% and 99% of the 1961-1990 average have increased in the last decade as have rainfall events exceeding 50mm. Both these trends point to an increase in frequency and intensity of rainfall across the UK.

Protecting your property from the risk of pluvial flooding is likely to become of increasing importance over the next decade and should form an important part of your purchasing decision. It is strongly advised that prior to committing to any property purchase you should investigate the insurance options on the property you intend to buy to see whether insurers are imposing additional premiums for the location under consideration as this will have an ongoing increased cost liability for you in years to come.

Your surveyor's independent survey report will identify the specific flood risk for the property you are intending to buy using official government data. It will also consider the situation of surrounding paths and surfaces to the property and how these may impact on these factors.

Theft

While nobody is going to steal your house, there will be features in the property which make it either more or less potentially prone to burglary or attempted intrusion.

1. Burglars target homes that they think will contain valuables. A sure giveaway is leaving packaging from expensive items outside your front door.

2. Burglars often look for homes with windows or doors left open or with vulnerable features that they can exploit.

3. Burglars are aware of the times when someone is expected to be away from their house such as during the school run or holidays.

4. Burglars typically do not want to be seen or heard and if they feel that they would be noticed by a neighbour or passer-by they are more likely to feel exposed and may move on to find somewhere else to burgle.

5. Burglars often choose a home because they've spotted a specific vehicle, motorcycle or bicycle they want to steal – and the keys are more than likely to be inside the residence.

6. Sheds and garages are often vulnerable as they are not that secure and contain tools which the burglar can use to assist them to gain entry to a home.

7. It's a fact that many burglars return to homes that they've previously burgled because the homeowner failed to upgrade security following the first burglary. They sometimes return to an area to try to burgle a nearby home that they spotted while committing a previous break in.

Even more reason for you to ensure you keep your home as 'safe as houses'.

So, how does your surveyor's independent survey report help you reduce the risk of theft from your property?

There are several factors that come into play. For example, if you have older double-glazed windows, they may well be more prone to attack as they were often fixed with externally beaded glazing units which can easily be removed from outside the property, allowing straightforward access into the building.

Old single-glazed timber windows, as well as requiring higher levels of maintenance than more modern aluminium or double-glazed PVC windows are also a weak point in the property and a straightforward point of forced entry.

Composite doors provide better levels of security than more basic UPVC doors which sometimes have a large base panel which can easily be pushed away, allowing for straightforward access into the property.

There is a current fashion towards the increasing use of video doorbell entry systems which can be very helpful in spotting potential intruders and deterring them. In the case of burglaries, the local police will sometimes make appeals to other local properties to see whether they have captured any images on their video door bells which may assist the police in capturing the criminals.

Good outside security lighting is also helpful in keeping your property safe. Criminals do not want to be seen or identified when attempting to approach the property.

Tall front hedges which help to maintain privacy to the property from people walking along the street can seem attractive but of course, this would be a great way for any potential intruder to keep their actions hidden away from the same passers-by. Any intended purchaser should be aware if the property has a footpath to the rear or side as this could have possible security issues.

All of the above factors would be noted and taken into consideration by the surveyor.

As your surveyors we look at property in a very different way to how an intending buyer would. We apply a professional eye and see things you would not notice.

MURKY DEPTHS AND HIDDEN TREASURES

L ike Davy Jones locker at the bottom of the sea, your new property can sometimes carry a few surprises and not always in a good way. Let's take a deeper look.

Murky Depths

In the UK today many first-time buyers enter the property market without an adequate understanding of the possible pitfalls they may and often do encounter when deciding how to find that 'dream home' they have always wanted. Their naivety and misplaced trust can lead them to proceed in completely the wrong way and then pay the price after they move in.

Typically, prospective buyers are given a limited amount of time to view the property on which they are expected to invest hundreds of thousands of pounds. An unsuspecting buyer can be drawn into this lifetime commitment without ever having somebody who knows about property actually inspect it and report to them.

As your surveyors, we see things that you do not because we look at properties in a very different way to the way the average buyer does. That means that we see the murky depths and the hidden treasures which you never do.

Cellars

Cellars are certainly a part of the property which can come under the heading of murky depths. The most common place to see a cellar is in a Victorian house where they may occupy a small area beneath the ground floor or in some cases occupy the whole of the footprint beneath the ground floor. Usually, they have limited head height although in some cases they do give the option to fully stand, making them an attractive option for conversion, in the opinion of some people.

Here at your surveyors we have inspected over 30,000 properties with many of them having a cellar. With that depth of experience, we can state that the vast majority of these are damp, albeit to varying degrees. It is a source of amusement when arriving at such a Victorian property for the vendor to state that "The cellar is very dry", when the reality on testing with a damp meter is usually completely the opposite.

Cellars are below the surrounding ground which means that the walls which form the cellar will be subject to hydrostatic pressure. This is where the pressure of the water in the surrounding ground pushes against the wall and over time will appear on the other side of the wall within the cellar itself. This brings some consequences. In particular, any timbers which are in contact with these damp walls are likely to rot. They will need to be cut away and then replaced, possibly given additional support and fully isolated from the damp cellar walls.

What is presented to you as a nice dry cellar is much more likely to require significant expenditure. Once identified, the repairs ought to be implemented with urgency. This is not only to upgrade the cellar for anything other than non-perishable storage but, more importantly, to protect the timbers which form the ground floor of the rooms above from decaying, deteriorating and in a worst case collapsing. The situation is often made even worse when vendors have decided to upgrade their "nice dry cellar" by boarding the walls and the underside of the floor joists above to create a den or study. This is often done without any attempt to resist the inevitable hydrostatic pressure and penetrating damp on the walls which have been boarded over. This in turn increases the risk of decay to any timbers bedded into the walls and any timber battens which may have been used behind the boarded walls to fix the boards to. Conditions have now been created where the decay could turn to dry rot. This is by far the most damaging type of decay which timber can suffer and is extremely disruptive and expensive to remedy.

Dry Rot

Dry rot (Serpula lacrymans) is a form of brown rot, a group of fungi which digest the cellulose and hemicellulose in timber. This particular species poses the greatest threat to buildings, since it can spread through non-nutrient providing materials (e.g., masonry and plaster) for several metres until it finds more timber to attack. Dry rot is spread by spores which are present in many buildings. The minimum moisture content of timber for spore germination is 28-30% (lower than other rots), and the relative humidity must be in excess of 95%.

Spores are resistant to desiccation and may still be viable for germination when they are several years old. If conditions are suitable the spores will germinate producing microscopic fungal threads called hyphae. This is why dry rot can spread so extensively. In essence, the murky depths of cellars should be treated with caution.
They were generally built for non-perishable storage including coal in many cases.

The old-fashioned method of carrying timber joists into the thickness of walls something which is not done today means that the average cellar will cost you money. Likely costs include remediating the risk of decay and cellars should continue to be left open, ventilated, and treated as suitable for non-perishable storage only in most cases.

Any previous attempts to have upgraded the cellar are in our experience likely to have failed or are likely to fail over time. This is because the lateral damp will continue to penetrate gradually through whatever efforts have been made to conceal it. These could be with boarding, or other forms of proprietary damp resistant specialist materials.

Underground Or Semi-Underground Garages

Other murky depths include underground or semi underground garages.

On sites where the land slopes upwards away from the front road, it is quite common to see that a garage has been constructed towards the front of the plot with direct access from the forward road. This would mean that all or part of the side and rear walls of the garage construction are below the level of the surrounding ground.

In effect, the garage becomes very similar to a cellar and the same issues are relevant in that there will be inevitable hydrostatic pressure for dampness to penetrate through the garage walls unless measures have been specifically designed to resist this.

Of course, in general, the damp resistant standards applied to garages are less rigorous than we would apply to our main home, and some elements of dampness in the garage even when constructed above ground are fairly normal. However, if you intend to store your highly cherished vintage car in the garage or anything which excessive moisture could damage then the question of dampness becomes much more critical.

Building a garage requires approval to confirm adequacy. Without independent confirmation of what was done it would not be possible to verify works that have been concealed. The first relevant regulations in their modern form were The Building

Regulations 1965 which came into operation in February 1966. Plans deposited in complying with the regulations should show what measures were undertaken to resist the risk of lateral penetrating damp. If the works were carried out in recent times you should also look to see whether there are insurance backed guarantees for these works to cover you for the cost of any future works should the damp resistant treatments fail, as remediation could be very expensive.

Your surveyors independent survey report would advise you on such matters and more. A recent extreme example of a below ground garage inspected by yoursurveyors.com showed that damp penetration had occurred for so long and to such a degree that the garage actually had stalactites growing down from its concrete ceiling and water running in rivulets down the walls. Interestingly, the vendors had told the intending purchasers when they inspected the property that they "couldn't find the keys for the garage" so they weren't able to inspect within it.

However, we insisted before arriving at the property that this would be necessary and suddenly, the secrets were revealed to all. The buyers withdrew. Nobody likes being misled.

Air Raid Shelters

Another example of murky depths although seen much less frequently now are air raid shelters in gardens. Originally these could have been the Anderson type shelter which was fabricated from sheets of corrugated metal and overlaid with earth, although most of these have now disappeared. However, occasionally we do see brick constructed air raid shelters which have been dug into the depths of the rear garden, with steps down into these from the main garden level. After around 80 years it is not surprising to note that when these are seen they have generally become quite hazardous. The steps leading down into them are usually very slippery and a particular hazard for young children who might come into contact with them. As there is likely to be no door directly into the shelter, this having rotted away many years ago, they often become a haven for creatures to rest or even nest in. The brickwork, itself, having been severely exposed to damp over such a lengthy period of time is prone to failure and in worst cases collapse.

As the potential buyer of the property, you are unlikely to even notice this on your time restricted inspection when thinking about buying, and because the cost of removal will be quite an expense, it is unlikely the vendors will point this out to you. This is another example of where your surveyor's independent survey report is so important.

Hidden Treasures

Hidden treasures, we must admit, are something as surveyors which we find rather less frequently. Occasionally though a property does throw up a peculiarity and this is part of what makes the surveyors job so interesting.

A while ago we inspected an extremely large property with a wealthy owner who clearly had things that they needed to keep safe and confidential. It became evident from the layout of the property that something was missing, and on questioning the owner they confirmed that they did in fact have a "secret room" which to that point neither the estate agent nor the buyer had been made aware of. They understood, of course, that we needed to inspect the whole of the property and so we were given access to this hidden room which we duly inspected in the usual manner in terms of its condition and in order to report to the client any defects. Fortunately, in this case there were no serious issues in this little corner of Narnia.

Maybe less of a hidden treasure but certainly a treasure, was the overall quality of a multi-million pound house we inspected in a location in the suburbs of London. The house was owned by a person who in general conversation with me shared the fact that they were diagnosed with obsessive compulsive disorder. This they did say was not something they would wish on their worst enemy which is a sad situation. However, the fact that they were so incredibly particular meant that many, in fact all, elements of the property they were selling were finished to a degree far and above the standards one would normally expect to see, and one feature remains with me to this day. They confirmed that the absolutely incredible internal doors with which the house was provided had been supplied and installed at a cost of over £2000 per individual door. When you consider the property had 42 of these doors, you can just imagine how much of a treasure the quality of this particular property was, throughout.

On a lighter note, with no pun intended, as you will see below a colleague who undertook refurbishment of neglected properties has on two separate occasions found £200 in notes tucked into the ceiling light fittings of properties where they were undertaking work. In both cases the notes had been there so long that they were no longer legal tender, but we are left to wonder why the same amount of money and why the same hiding place?

Sitting somewhere between a hidden treasure and a murky depth I am reminded of a modified staircase which I saw many years ago. The owner had cut out panels from all of the risers and the newel post and handrail, inserted mixed red, blue and green plastic into the holes created and then proceeded to install lights beneath the plastic, so that when he reached to a switch under the stairs and flicked it on, the whole staircase lit up like a hideous kaleidoscope. I shall never forget when he proudly announced to me that he had "seen this in a nightclub in Muswell Hill many years ago!". I don't think he understood that it would not transfer happily into a three bedroom semi-detached property in the suburbs and I had to report to my client that one of the first jobs they would need to do would be to cut out and replace the whole staircase at a cost of several thousand pounds.

PLANTS THAT HEAL, PLANTS THAT KILL

A beautifully planted garden can be a delight and, when looking for a property, it is easy to be drawn to a cottage with roses round the door or a lovely ivy or wisteria adorning the walls. The thought of sitting in the garden on a summer's day under the dappled shade of a mature tree sipping an iced drink can be the charm that influences your decision on whether to buy that property or not. However, there is a downside to nature's bounty. Your surveyor's report will bring to your attention concerns that you probably never considered.

Trees

On average an adult tree absorbs approximately 25kgs of CO_2 per year so making a positive contribution to reducing CO_2 emissions. Trees help to stop flooding and landslides. Leaves and branches can retain rainfall, so it disperses at a gentler rate. They can reduce temperature improving summer comfort in nearby buildings, producing a natural sunscreen by providing shade. However, problems can arise from trees adjacent to your property. Despite the many benefits of trees, their relationship to buildings is one to be carefully considered. Relevant factors include the type of tree, is it mature or immature and what is its distance and orientation from the property. The type of building construction and the type of subsoil can also have an effect.

Your surveyor's independent survey will address these issues for you and allow you to make an informed decision about your property purchase. Nobody else other than your surveyor is available to advise you in this way. It may be that you have plans to remove a certain tree after you move in. However, a TPO (Tree Preservation Order) may legally prevent you from doing this. A fine of up to £20,000 can be imposed for destroying or cutting down a protected tree without permission. In some local authority areas, there can be "blanket" TPOs, meaning any tree with a trunk over quite a modest diameter could be protected.

A TPO could potentially impact on any future plans you may have for a conservatory or extension. Even if you are allowed to cut down a tree, doing so on the wrong type of subsoil could damage your building by "heave", a structural problem which can take years to solve. This would make your new property unsaleable in the meantime and your insurance invalid if you caused the problem.

The shedding of leaves by deciduous trees in autumn can block gutters and downpipes leading to overflows and damp and also damaging your property in other ways. The root systems of trees can and frequently do damage underground drains and uplift garden walls, which if next to a public footpath or pavement could leave you open to legal liabilities for injury or damage if they failed and hurt a passer-by.

Your surveyors independent survey report will identify the subsoil, point out trees of relevance and give general and legal advice and guidance on any issues which may arise. Your surveyor is the only qualified, technical professional to visit and assess the property on your behalf.

Japanese Knotweed (Fallopia Japonica)

Probably the most incorrectly reported and ludicrously

demonised plant of recent times.

Nonetheless, false hysteria created by mortgage lenders and others has given rise to a situation with this simple plant which needs consideration because of the way it has been incorrectly described. This has promoted the growth by contractors of an industry geared to charging the homeowner for hugely expensive treatment plans and whose sole purpose, some may say, appears to be to increase the profits of those same contractors.

The most recent and extensive research to date, a 2018 study by global infrastructure services firm AECOM and the University of Leeds, found no evidence that Japanese knotweed is especially damaging when compared to other plants. AECOM's principal ecologist, the aptly named Dr Mark Fennell, said: *"We found nothing to suggest that Japanese knotweed causes significant damage to buildings – even when it is growing in close proximity – and certainly no more damage than other species that are not subject to such strict lending policies."*

This is in stark contrast to the alarmist warnings in the public domain which include claims that knotweed can cause massive damage to house foundations. Co-author of the research, Dr Karen Bacon of Leeds University is quick to refute this, stating: *"This plant poses less of a risk to buildings and other structures than many woody species, particularly trees. It is capable of damaging built structures, but where this occurs it is usually because an existing weakness or defect has been exacerbated."*

The 2018 findings tally with an earlier report in 2012 by the Royal Institution of Chartered Surveyors (RICS), which concluded that Japanese knotweed was 'treatable and rarely causes severe damage to the property'. The 2018 study also found that Japanese knotweed rhizomes (the root system) rarely extend more than 4m from the visible plants, and usually spread less than 2.5m. This is much less than the 7 metres commonly cited as the risk zone.

Despite these facts the industry remains out of touch and having a professional assess the risk at the property on your behalf remains a necessity. The presence of Japanese knotweed can have a significantly negative impact on mortgageability and saleability.

It could deem the property unmortgageable, particularly in the absence of an insurance backed treatment plan. It can take five years or more to eradicate Japanese knotweed and treatment plans can be expensive.

Since 2013 a property seller is required to state whether Japanese Knotweed is present on their property through a TA form – the property information form used for conveyancing. There have been many occasions whereby the answer to that question has been "no", yet Japanese Knotweed has been found within the boundaries.

Your surveyor is the best placed to advise you whether there are any indications of Japanese Knotweed to consider on your property purchase.

Ivy And Other Climbers

A climbing wall plant can be very attractive, but as a rule they can be problematic.

Plants like moisture. Of course they do, they need it to survive. Buildings on the other hand are designed to keep moisture and damp out. Plants sitting on a building therefore create a dichotomy, between wanting to attract moisture and needing to repel water. Climbers like ivy are a concern for this reason and for another reason.

The suckers which hold them in place can encourage and widen fine cracks in brickwork and render which will then retain moisture. This not only makes the building more susceptible to condensation internally, but it will also freeze the retained water in colder months which then expands and worsens the cracks until eventually render or mortar falls off making the situation progressively worse.

The sort of plants to avoid are those that trail up your wall. These are often the ones that have "suckers" or little mini branches like spikes, that burrow under the paint or pebbledash, into the render of the wall for a foothold. Ivy is a prime example. Excessive growth can obstruct important ventilation grills for floors or to walls generally and we have seen them entangle in boiler flues with serious health risks because of this. Another point to bear in mind is that as plants grow on buildings, they can potentially provide a pathway for creatures into your open windows and mice for example could go on to create some damage internally.

Bamboo, Hogweed And More

There are many other plants to be aware of when buying a property.

Giant hogweed which is a close relative of cow parsley and can reach over 10 feet in height. In some cases when allowed to continue growing it has reached 20 feet. More often seen in spring to autumn, giant hogweed is best treated in summer. The sap of giant hogweed contains highly toxic chemicals known as photosensitising furanocoumarins. These are extremely sensitive to light. If this sap comes in to contact with skin, it can cause a reaction which causes very nasty burns to the skin.

Bamboo is not classed as an invasive species in the Wildlife and Countryside Act 1981 and there are currently no restrictions on planting it. However, bamboo can also spread out of control if not monitored properly. Encroachment cases are becoming more common. Homeowners are increasingly taking legal action against neighbours who have allowed bamboo to spread. Some varieties can spread up to 30ft if left unchecked and can quickly encroach onto neighbouring properties resulting in disputes and costly legal bills.

There are many garden plants with mostly low levels of toxicity, however, if you have children or even curious pet prone to chewing who knows what in the garden, it would be worth taking extra care with these and other plants you may commonly see in UK gardens...

* Water hemlock
* Laburnum
* Rhododendron
* Angel's trumpet
* Belladonna
* Foxglove
* Elephant ear
* Poison ivy
* Philodendron
* Oleander
* Daffodil
* Lily-of-the-valley
* Ficus
* Desert rose

Moss

Most people are familiar with moss. Gardeners are often keen to eliminate it from their manicured lawns, whilst others actively encourage its growth because of properties it brings to the garden. Mosses function like sponges using their capillary spaces to hang on to water. They help to soak up rainfall, maintain moisture in the soil below and keep conditions around them humid. This enables other plants around them to thrive in habitats such as marshes and woodland.

On buildings however moss and lichens, often found close together are more of an enemy than a friend. Lichens are actually made up of two or more different organisms. These exist in a mutually beneficial relationship called symbiosis. Accumulations of moss are often seen on the surfaces of roof tiles or slates. Some think this adds character to a property. What it actually adds is retention of damp.

Buildings and their components are designed to repel damp. Moss on roof tiles encourages concrete or clay tiles to hold on to moisture longer. This in turn will cause damp to penetrate through the tiles leading to high damp readings on the timber battens below which support them. This, in time will cause decay in these battens leading to the tiles slipping and falling away from the roof.

Moss on the surfaces of the tiles will create an acidic run off from the tiles which in turn will encourage decay and rust in any cast iron rainwater goods which of course can lead to saturation of the walls below and consequential damage internally. Another area in which this can be a problem is in older properties with cast iron or lead lined guttering and rainwater pipes. Such properties are often situated in a conservation area which would restrict changing to more modern plastic equivalents. Accumulations of moss in guttering can also reduce the capacity of the gutters, meaning that in even modest rainfall they may well overflow, again damaging and saturating elements of the building below.

Moss and lichen growth can often occur on timber decking if it is neglected. Decking with moss on the surface due to retained moisture encourages rot and decay on the deck boarding itself. This in turn can lead to a risk of trips and falls and future financial outlay to cover the cost of repair or replacement due to damage. Timber decking is often installed in an amateur way without proper consideration of how the support structure beneath the boarding needs to be protected from damp and rot coming from below.

Your surveyor's independent survey report will bring together

all the elements which can impact on your purchasing decision and the costs that you may face when buying a property. These include not only the main constructional elements of the building itself, but also, as shown above the ways in which these interact with nature.

SERIOUS HEALTH RISKS

The changing face of property construction over the last 100 years or more has sometimes come with a longer term health implication. It is really important to be aware of all such issues.

Asbestos

Asbestos is the name given to six minerals that naturally occur in the environment as bundles of fibres that can be separated into thin, durable threads. These fibres are resistant to heat, fire, and chemicals and do not conduct electricity. For these reasons asbestos has been used widely in many industries over the years and particularly in commercial and residential buildings.

However, the importation, supply and use of all asbestos has been banned in the UK since 1999. This is because of the health risk associated with breathing in asbestos fibres. When damaged asbestos releases fibres which can be breathed in and swallowed. Breathing in asbestos fibres can lead to a condition called asbestosis that leads to an increased susceptibility to cancer (mesothelioma). Asbestos has been classified as being carcinogenic to humans.

If products or materials containing asbestos are disturbed for example, drilled, sawed nailed or cut, this will release asbestos fibres into the air. If these fibres are breathed in, they may get trapped in the lungs and remain there for a long time. Over time, these fibres can accumulate and cause scarring and inflammation to the lung tissue and consequentially having a negative effect on breathing and can lead to serious health implications.

Research shows no amount of asbestos exposure is safe. The risk of developing mesothelioma is highest among asbestos workers who endured years of exposure, but it also can develop in people with limited exposure. Symptoms of mesothelioma do not show up until 20-60 years after asbestos exposure.

Exposure to asbestos causes most "mesotheliomas" which is a type of cancer that develops in the lining that covers the outer surface of some of the body's organs. NHS UK advises that this type of diagnosis is usually linked to asbestos exposure. Mesothelioma can typically take more than 20 years to develop after exposure to asbestos.

The Health and Safety Executive state that as long as asbestos is in good condition and is not disturbed or damaged then there is negligible risk.

Asbestos containing materials are pretty much only dangerous if they are damaged or disturbed as previously mentioned, as this is when the harmful asbestos fibres are released into the atmosphere and can be inhaled, posing a serious risk to health.

Asbestos fibres may become damaged or disturbed if carrying out routine DIY, maintenance, or renovation work in homes. This can even include tasks like redecoration works, hanging pictures or installing new light fittings as any of these simple tasks could potentially disturb existing asbestos in homes.

You should make yourself aware about potential asbestos in your home if you plan on doing any kind of DIY or renovations which could cause potential damage to any asbestos containing materials. Your surveyor's report will highlight to you any potential asbestos containing materials that could be present at the home you intend to purchase. With this information, you must then contact a licensed asbestos removal company, part of The Asbestos Removal Contractors Association to carry out an asbestos identification survey and to test the potential asbestos containing materials. Asbestos testing involves analysing the asbestos containing materials to determine whether they contain any asbestos and if they do what type.

Testing involves taking single or bulk samples of the suspected materials and having them analysed for asbestos fibres in an independent laboratory. The results will confirm whether the materials contain asbestos and will confirm the type if necessary.

Under some circumstances, certain low risk asbestos containing materials that are in good condition can be encapsulated, which means concealing them with a protective layer to prevent the materials from being damaged and releasing dangerous fibres.

Asbestos encapsulation tends to be more cost effective than removal and can be carried out with minimal disturbance. However, there is still always a concealed risk and removal is the safest and best option, not only for your safety but for the safety of future potential purchasers of the building.

Where Is Asbestos Typically Found In Properties?

* Gutters and downpipes
* Soffit boards
* Exterior window panels
* Roof coverings
* Drainage pipes
* Water tanks
* Pipe lagging
* Insulation
* Textured decorative coating eg. artex
* Ceiling boards/tiles

* Bath panels
* Toilet seat and cistern
* Heat insulating boards
* Thermoplastic floor tiles
* Dated heating components
And more...

Mould And Condensation

It has become a well-known health risk that occupants of a damp or mouldy building are at an increased risk of experiencing health problems. People react differently to exposure with some people being more sensitive to mould than others. Problems such as respiratory symptoms and infections, allergic rhinitis and asthma are examples of the health implications people have faced as a result.

According to NHS UK babies, children, the elderly, those with existing skin problems, respiratory problems and weakened immune systems should stay away from damp and mould. Moulds produce allergens, irritants and sometimes toxic substances. Inhaling or touching mould spores may cause an allergic reaction, such as sneezing, a runny nose, red eyes and skin rash. Moulds can also cause asthma attacks.

Mould and damp are produced by excess moisture. Moisture can develop within buildings in many ways including excessive moisture production and a lack of ventilation, leaking pipes, rising damp in basements and ground floor accommodation, penetrating damp due to damaged roof coverings, windows or defective external building fabric allowing dampness to penetrate the walls and appear internally. Newly built homes are generally still damp during their drying out phase.

To summarise, the principal causes of mould and damp within a building are:

1. Condensation

2. Defective pipes

3. Penetrating dampness

4. Rising dampness

Condensation generally occurs when warm air meets cold surfaces or if there is too much humidity. When moisture-packed warm air comes into contact with a cold surface, it cools down quickly and releases the water, which turns into liquid droplets on the surface.

Polystyrene

Polystyrene is a highly flammable or easily ignited product. Polystyrene ceiling tiles and coving are not illegal, and you can still go to stockists and DIY stores to buy them. Modern products however, contain a fire retardant additive and are not so high a risk as older materials.

As with many products these had a particular popularity a few years ago and as with all fashions many people followed the trend. It is not uncommon to see them on ceilings still in many properties.

Fire in property at any time is a risk to occupants and if a fire occurs, the last thing you would want is for the risk to the occupiers to be made even worse by the presence of polystyrene tiles or wall linings.

You may ask the question why were these materials used in properties in the first place?

Most commonly they were used as a basic form of insulation, partly to assist keeping heat within the property, although when used as wall linings on the external walls, these are an indicator of the likelihood that condensation issues were being experienced. Polystyrene linings were provided to mitigate against this problem.

The insulating properties of the polystyrene was used to slightly raise the surface temperature of the walls over which it was applied, and in raising this surface temperature, it would have reduced the risk of condensation appearing on the surface of the wall as it would have moved the dew point to a different position within the structure.

Dew point is the atmospheric temperature (varying according to pressure and humidity) below which water droplets begin to condense and condensation can form.

Controlling the risk of condensation needs consideration of the interaction between insulation, surface temperatures, moisture production, background heating and ventilation.

Your surveyors independent survey report will advise you on such matters and give advice on possible options which could be followed to improve the situation.

Lead Pipes

Lead dissolving into drinking water from lead pipes can be harmful if it builds up in the body – especially for babies and children, whose development can be affected.

The use of lead in plumbing has been banned in the UK for more than 25 years, and houses built before 1970 are the most likely to have lead pipes. However, newer homes are not entirely safe. Lead solder used for jointing copper pipes as a low-cost alternative by DIY enthusiasts or unqualified plumbers can also put drinking water at risk. Exposure to lead can be harmful to our health, especially for unborn babies and young children, so it's important to keep lead levels in drinking water low.

Children absorb more lead than adults due to their growing bones and other organs which lead can become deposited in. Although children are at increased risk of the effects of lead poisoning, exposure via drinking contaminated water can also result in illness in adults.

Your surveyor's independent survey report will advise you of the presence or risk of lead pipes within the property.

Gas

Who is competent to work on gas fittings?

In domestic properties this must be carried out by someone on the Gas Safe Register who is qualified to work on gas appliances. It is illegal for an unregistered person to carry out work on any domestic gas appliance. You can check this by contacting the Gas Safe Register.

All those who are registered, are required to carry a Gas Safe ID card, which shows the type of work they are qualified to do and whether their qualifications are up to date.

Working with gas appliances is difficult, specialised and potentially very dangerous. Only competent engineers should attempt it. If unregistered workers try to bypass the law, they are not only putting themselves at risk of prosecution and a large fine or even imprisonment they are also putting their customers' lives at risk.

A Gas Safety Certificate ensures that a property is safe and secure in terms of gas appliances and connections. A Gas Safety inspection involves an examination of all your gas appliances and connections by a Gas Safe registered engineer to make sure everything is working correctly.

Electrics

Where would we be without our electricity supply? Modern living means we fill our homes with ever more electric gadgets and gizmos, so it has never been more important to make sure that the electricity supply in your home does not fall short of the necessary standards.

The main hazards associated with electricity are electric shock and burns from contact with live parts, injury from exposure to arcing, fire from faulty electrical equipment or installations and explosion caused by unsuitable electrical apparatus or static electricity igniting flammable vapours or dusts.

Other causes for concern include:

1. Poor wiring which can increase the chances of fires, power surges, and other serious consequences.

2. Outlets close to water.

3. Lightbulbs near flammable materials.

4. Covered electrical cords and wires.

5. Too many and trailing wire extension leads.

6. Fittings likely to be touched by wet hands.

7. Amateur unsafe changes to electrical installations.

8. Inadequately protected electrical supplies externally.

You should ensure that you receive and keep the paperwork for all completed electrical installation work and periodic inspection and testing. All certificates and reports should include schedules of inspections and test results. The type of certification or report you receive depends on the extent and type of electrical installation work, or inspection and testing, that you have had carried out.

Electrical Installation Certificates (EICs) and Minor Electrical Installation Works Certificates (MEIWCs) provide you, as the person responsible for the safety of an electrical installation with a declaration that the new installation, or alteration or addition, is safe to use at the time it was put into service.

Keeping hold of these certificates also provides a basis for any further inspection and testing, as they can help save on costly exploratory work which might otherwise be needed in future. Additionally, in the event of a claim that injury or fire was caused by an electrical installation, certificates are documentary evidence which help show that the installation had been installed to a satisfactory standard of safety which could be extremely important in the event of making an insurance claim for fire damage.

Radon

Radon is a colourless, odourless radioactive gas. It is formed by the radioactive decay of the small amounts of uranium that occur naturally in all rocks and soils. Radioactive elements decay and emit radiation. Any exposure to this type of radiation is a risk to health. Radiation is a form of energy and can cause damage in living tissues increasing the risk of cancer.

Radon is everywhere; formed from the uranium in all rocks and soils. Outdoors everywhere and indoors in many areas the radon levels are low and the risk to health is small.

The amount of radon is measured in becquerels per cubic metre of air (Bq m-3). The average level in UK homes is 20 Bq m-3. For levels below 100 Bq m-3, your individual risk remains relatively low and not a cause for concern. However, the risk increases as the radon level increases.

Radioactivity is where unstable elements, such as naturally occurring uranium, thorium and radon, break down resulting in energy being released and different elements formed. The new elements may also be unstable so the process is repeated until a stable element is formed. The energy given off is called radiation and can be alpha or beta particles or gamma rays. Alpha particles are more harmful than beta particles or gamma rays. This is because alpha particles contain more energy and are absorbed over a smaller area.

We are all exposed to radiation from natural and man-made sources. Just 20 Bq m-3 (the average radon level in UK homes) gives us half our exposure to radiation from all sources. Higher radon levels give higher exposures. That is why it is important to find out the levels in your home.

There is a publicly available online map on ukradon.org where you can search by postcode to establish the risk of radon in that area.

The darker the colour on the radon maps, the greater the chance of a high radon level in a building. However not all buildings, even in the darkest areas, have high levels.

Specific property testing is required to establish the actual radon levels in any given property.

Legionnaires Disease

Legionellosis is a collective term for diseases caused by legionella bacteria including the most serious, Legionnaires' disease, as well as the similar but less serious conditions of Pontiac fever and Lochgoilhead fever.

Legionnaires' disease is a potentially fatal form of pneumonia, and everyone is susceptible to infection.

The bacterium Legionella pneumophila and related bacteria are common in natural water sources such as rivers, lakes and reservoirs, but usually in low numbers. They may also be found in hot and cold-water systems.

If conditions are favourable, the bacteria may grow increasing the risks of Legionnaires' disease and it is therefore important to control the risks by introducing appropriate measures.

Stagnant water favours Legionella growth. To reduce the risk you should remove dead legs/dead ends in pipe-work, flush out infrequently used outlets (including showerheads and taps) at least weekly and clean and de-scale shower heads and hoses at least quarterly.

7 THINGS TO NEVER DO

Buying property can be a wonderful experience enriching your life. There are however pitfalls along the way and here we help you avoid them.

Buying At Auction

The plethora of television programmes broadcast at the present time which imply how easy it is to make money out of property and how buying at auction is the clever way to purchase is a worrying trend.

Yes, you can sometimes bag a bargain at auctions, but you need to bear in mind that everybody there is also seeking that same bargain. You will probably be in competition with prospective buyers with greater knowledge and experience who have been through the process on more than one occasion and have a better understanding of the true market value of the properties up for auction.

There will also be prospective buyers lacking in that knowledge and experience who are unable to assess what is a bargain at auction. They may well get caught up in the excitement of bidding for a property and end up paying too much or buying a property not suited to their needs or budgetary limitations.

That could be you.

There are lots of reasons why properties end up for sale at auction but undoubtedly one of the most common is because it has been difficult to sell that property through the normal method of private treaty.

Properties in auction will often have all manner of issues which would mean that offering them for sale to the general public could be problematic, as prospective buyers would need to obtain a mortgage to purchase them. Historically, this is why in the past most properties at auction would have been sold to cash buyers.

As previously mentioned, a belief has grown amongst the general public that buying at auction means buying a bargain. However, this is not always the case.

Before even considering attending an auction you should carefully study the conditions of sale of any property you are interested in as these will be binding if you proceed to making an offer on the property. Additionally, you will be required to produce a large deposit on the date of the auction.

It is imperative that you have previously obtained your surveyor's independent survey report on the property so that you can be positive about its condition and any shortcomings or factors which might make subsequent resale difficult.

Some recently published information regarding auctions suggested that you should have the property inspected by a builder or handyman so that you know it's condition before you commit to the purchase.

This is terrible advice.

Property inspections need to be undertaken by a fully qualified, experienced residential surveyor who will give you information on all manner of possible restrictions or limitations about the property rather than just telling you how much it will cost to replace some windows and redecorate.

For example, is the property of non-traditional construction? Such properties are unlikely to be eligible for a mortgage upon resale. Does the property have large areas of single skin brick construction? As above, such properties would face difficulty in getting mortgage approval upon resale. Are there issues within the curtilage or within the influencing distance on adjacent land of Japanese knotweed? Such issues would also restrict the possibility of a future sale. Are there issues of prescriptive rights, boundary encroachments, works undertaken without regulatory compliance or indeed, a myriad of other issues?

All these issues would be covered in your surveyor's independent survey report.

If any of these issues were found to be present, your surveyor would give you clear information and advice on the appropriate action to take long before you attend the auction.

Another term which you may come across is when properties are quoted as being sold by "modern method of auction". We have seen several slightly different ways in which this is approached and differences in the relevant contractual positions but in essence it means that the onus is on the purchaser of the property to pay the estate agents or auctioneers fees, on top of all the other expenses they are already faced with when buying a property.

It is extremely important to confirm exactly what your position in relation to such purchasing fees is and to be certain that you will not ever be charged any fees if you decide not to proceed with the purchase for any reason at all.

It is imperative to legally confirm that you as the purchaser have control over the factors which are an acceptable reason for not proceeding and not being charged any fees and that this decision is in no way left to the selling agent or auction company.

Unless you are 100% clear about what buying at auction entails and the correct way that you should proceed this is often the wrong option to consider.

That "Nice" Extension

Most of us love an extension. The most common form of extension is the single storey addition to the rear of the property, usually to enlarge the kitchen and create a lovely large new open kitchen diner. This can be a wonderful thing if it is done properly but so often it is not.

This is a problem we see hundreds of times every year and one which so many people seem to be blissfully unaware of. Because people want to get the maximum benefit from their extension it is natural to try and provide the maximum amount of additional floor area. In order to achieve this, it is tempting take the extension to the full width of the rear of the property. Superficially this does sound like a good idea. However, this approach is often taken when using a concrete floor for the new extension. If this then joins onto a timber ground floor which formed the original sections of the property to which the extension has been added, problems may arise.

Timber floors must have through ventilation.

Typically, this means that air bricks will be provided to the front and rear of a timber ground floor which allows the throughput of air ensuring that there is no risk of any build-up of stagnant pockets of air and moisture within the timber floor. Placing an extension concrete floor fully across the rear of a property is often done without correctly continuing this airbrick ventilation through the concrete floor by using ducting to ensure that the required throughput of freshening air is maintained.

Blocking rear air bricks in this way creates a situation where, over time, the lack of through ventilation and the build-up of stagnant moist air can create fungal decay to the now blocked timbers in the original ground floor. In an older property this situation can be made much worse if the inevitable gradual breakdown of the damp proof course in the walls creates rising damp which when coupled with inadequate ventilation and timber floors are the perfect conditions to allow dry rot to form. Eliminating this problem can be very disruptive and often very expensive. When you consider that in many instances the whole situation could have been avoided by a competent builder correctly installing ducting and through ventilation during construction, it is disappointing that we see the situation occur repeatedly.

Don't believe that because an extension has been constructed with regulatory compliance that all the required associated technical matters such as through ventilation will have been dealt with properly. This is very frequently not the case.

Another concern to take into consideration with extensions is whether the need for inevitable future maintenance was considered when the extension was being built?

So often we look with despair at extensions which have been added to a property leaving a gap of just a few centimetres between the walls of the extension and an adjoining structure. How on earth do people imagine it would be possible to repair and maintain the walls of the building when all you can do is look at them through a tiny gap? How is it physically possible to maintain the building when it is necessary. It is analogous to designing a new car where the only access to maintain the engine is through one of the tiny air vents in the dashboard.

The cost of buying property comprises three things. The cost to purchase, the cost to repair and the cost to maintain. If you cannot access part of the property to maintain it, then you are certainly storing up headaches and increased costs for the future.

Movement And Distortion

Should you buy a house which has suffered previous structural movement or has been underpinned? If everything required in such circumstances has been dealt with properly then there need be no reason for you not to proceed with the purchase of such a dwelling. However, the questions that do arise are; has everything been dealt with correctly and what situation has the property been subsequently left in?

Your surveyor's independent survey report will guide you carefully through the various technical and procedural steps which should have been followed if a property has been either simply monitored in terms of possible structural movement or has then gone on to require structural repair and underpinning because of movement.

However, there is a further step to always consider with this which is how much movement has been left in the property following structural monitoring or repair?

Many people buy properties which have been underpinned providing they have been satisfied in accordance with their surveyor's recommendations that all the correct steps have been followed. However, movement in a property usually creates distortion to differing elements and in differing extent. Some distortion and unevenness in properties is often considered to be part of the character, and certainly in 15th or 16th century historic timber framed houses the degree of distortion is way above that which one would accept in properties of more modern eras. When structural movement occurs in properties it will frequently take the extent of unevenness and out of true to a level at which serviceability in the property can become affected.

What this means is that even though a property may have been professionally underpinned and carries full certification, warranties and insurances, it may still be a problem for saleability if the works undertaken did not correct excess distortion internally and externally within the various elements of the building.

Consider, for a moment, a property which has suffered previous structural movement on one side, leaving floors distorted and falling away to that side. Whilst the problem of movement in the property may have been corrected by underpinning, if the floors have not been re-levelled then this would almost certainly deter many purchasers and levelling floors is not as straightforward as it may seem. Certainly, new joists could be installed or firring pieces applied on top of joists to restore the surface of any particular floor to the level position. This can however impact on the skirtings in the room and on the doors, door frames and openings and the way that any floor relevelled interacts with other floors in other rooms in the property.

Each part of a building is intrinsically linked with other parts, so whilst purchasing an underpinned property is not in itself necessaryily a bad thing, it is imperative to obtain the correct professional advice to ensure everything required has been properly attended to and that you are satisfied with the buildings current structural condition.

Love Thy Neighbour

Neighbours come in many forms. We all think of our neighbours as the people who live next door and of course that is true, but when it comes to buying property, neighbours are not always in human form, and they're not always next door either, but they can still impact on whether you should buy a property.

Sewage treatment plants are an integral part of modern life and they pop up all over the place. However, they can leave a lingering unpleasant odour. If the property you are thinking about buying is potentially downwind of such a plant, this could impact on whether or not it is a good idea to purchase there. Even if you think you know an area it's a good idea to do a bit of local research on what is around the property.

Sewage treatment plants are one example but even in relatively urban areas you can come across pig farms, abattoirs, scrapyards, excavation works and more. These are all things which can reduce the price of the property, making it seem more attractive to buy but will similarly not only reduce its price when you come to sell but will limit your marketability options.

As for the human neighbours look carefully particularly at what is either side of the property you intend to purchase. You cannot control the actions of your neighbours. If they have an untidy or unruly appearing house or garden overgrown with brambles and weeds or half dismantled cars as a forward aspect this is likely to be a continuing problem. You can do your best to turn your own property into a palace but if you have a wreck next door it will make selling the property on a difficult task in the future.

Something people often overlook is that none of us can predict our future.

We can never be sure our 'forever' home will actually stay as such or whether circumstances such as poor health, family matters, job situations and the like could mean we need to move on much more quickly than originally anticipated. If you have purchased a home without considering restrictive future sale factors, this could have serious and stressful consequences if the need to move the property on swiftly suddenly arises.

Doubtful Diy

Your surveyors will almost certainly have seen many DIY "palaces" over the years. Some people are indeed very good at improving and modernising their own homes.

They may not be a qualified tradesman, but they can still have ability in that respect and providing they know their limitations and when to call in an expert, improvements can add value.

Sadly, more often we see people who with good intentions have undertaken works without the proper understanding of how things should be done, how components interact and in many cases how regulatory compliance is essential and must be complied with. Attending an evening class and buying a cordless drill is unlikely to compensate for the lack of professional capability.

It is also important to appreciate that many of the works undertaken on properties by suitably qualified tradespeople will and should be offered with long-term insurance backed guarantees to confirm the capability of the individuals and to provide a warranty to the intending purchaser that if any defects occur, they will have an insurance policy on which to claim for rectification costs.

Doubtful DIY won't be offering any warranties or insurances and if a "friend" has carried out the work for cash you could be left high and dry with inadequacies causing further long-term complications and, in some cases, leading to higher costs than if the work had been done correctly in the first place.

Your surveyor's independent survey report will always point you in the right direction as to what has been done, how it should have been done, by whom it should have been done and whether insurance backed guarantees and warranties specifically for those works and fully transferable to you on completion should be in place.

No Service Charges

How appealing does it sound when you see a flat being offered for sale with no service charges whatsoever when others are quoting £2000 or £3000 per year for a service charge?

Don't be fooled. No service charges on the building where there are inevitably elements of shared responsibility generally means nobody is maintaining the building.

You will hear it said that repair costs are simply shared between the owners as and when the need arises. So, consider the situation where a block of flats needs a new roof costing £30,000 and there are five different owners of flats in the building all suddenly being asked to pay £6000 each for the repairs which are becoming increasingly urgent. Most people don't have that amount of money lying around and depending on their individual circumstances may be unable to raise that money at all.

So where does that leave the situation? Either the owners who do have the money have to pay their share and somebody else's share or the works don't get done and the building continues to deteriorate. In the meantime, all the owners of the flats in the building will have extreme difficulty in selling their properties because of this.

Flats require maintenance charges which should be adequate and should run alongside a programme of planned future maintenance. There should be an annual sinking fund into which monies are paid over many years to ensure that when large capital items of expenditure arise these will have been planned for by collecting the service charges over the previous years.

No service charges or an inadequately capitalised annual sinking fund with no programme of planned future maintenance is often a big negative when considering purchasing properties with shared liabilities.

Assume Access

With most property purchases access is fairly straightforward. In most cases properties sit on a plot which joins a road which is owned and maintained by the local authority and for which charges are in effect payable through local taxes.

Sometimes though there are variations to this.

Take for example the situation where several properties sit on a private road where ownership of and maintenance on is not devolved to the local authority. Whilst there are adequate provisions confirming that everybody is permitted access across this and if there are clear allocations of liability for repair and maintenance and there is a fund gradually accumulating for the inevitability of future repairs then this can become a desirable part of a properties appeal.

Problems can arise though if there is not absolute clarity on such matters. Although rare it is possible that a situation can arise where even though access may have been used for many years across an area of private land, this access might be denied when ownership of surrounding areas and properties changes.

New owners suddenly realising they have some exclusivity of rights and access may not be so generous in permitting others to use the access without creating some form of charge.

Also, even if the access position is adequately confirmed by your legal advisors, it is important to also consider what is the condition of the access way now and what happens should this deteriorate either gradually or suddenly, for example in the situation where a sinkhole might suddenly open up beneath the ground.

In that situation there would be a need to immediately repair the access and the cost could be very significant. If there are no specific provisions for this then there could be difficulties in getting everybody to pay towards the cost, especially those who perhaps are less affected depending on exactly the position of the damage itself.

Furthermore, if the costs are significant then some may be unwilling or even unable to contribute to the repair costs and this creates an invidious situation all of which certainly needs addressing before committing to any potential purchase where such situations could occur.

Private road access can seem very desirable, but it is imperative that your legal advisors investigate fully such situations to your entire satisfaction before committing to exchange of contracts.

EXTENSION WOES

If there is one thing most people love when it comes to property, it's an extension. They come in all shapes and sizes. Single storey, two storey, side extensions, rear extensions, wrap around extensions, rooms in the roof space, converted garages and sometimes even converted cellars or upgraded conservatories.

There is a belief however that is not always correct, that adding an extension to your property will increase the value by more than the cost of the extension itself and that it will make it more saleable and attractive to the general market. Often you will see properties advertised as having extension potential. However, this is often without any consideration of the many and varied factors which may limit the option to extend, or which might provide technical restrictions on what you can or cannot do to the existing building.

An extension will have a major effect on your home, garden and neighbours and may well need building regulation approval even if it does not necessarily need planning permission. In drawing up plans you will need to look at a variety of possible problems. What would be the effect on access to your home and garden, could there be a problem with movement in and around your home and might there be a negative effect on the natural light in existing rooms?

You will also need to consider what building materials to use, particularly if your home was built using unusual construction techniques or materials such as steel framed or concrete houses. In addition if an extension is planned for two or more storeys, the plans will also need to cover stairs, handrails and balustrades, sound proofing, particularly in any sleeping accommodation and provision for fire escape from upper floors.

Building over or near a public sewer requires that you meet the stipulations of the water authority to avoid damage. These stipulations can vary between authorities but broadly you need to apply to see if you need a "build over agreement".

There are two types of pipes that need to be taken into account.

> *Sewers: Which carry wastewater from two or more houses and which are within your property boundary.*

> *Lateral drains: Which carry wastewater from a single house and meet the public sewer network outside the boundary of that house.*

No inspection chambers on your property doesn't necessarily mean there aren't pipes concealed underground. Your local water company should be approached to confirm if any of the above exist. Proposed or existing construction must comply or must have complied. Failure of compliance could result in a need for additional works at your cost. Appropriate access for maintenance is always required. Inspection chambers to achieve this may be internal in which case appropriate double sealed screwed access covers are needed. Where existing construction appears to be over drains it is especially important to confirm full compliance prior to purchase commitment.

There are some exceptions where regulatory permissions are not required such as for conservatories up to a certain size, small detached buildings within the boundaries of the land and small porches, again up to a certain size. There are still restrictions on what you can and cannot do with and without regulatory compliance. The safest option is always to approach your local building control and planning authorities to confirm the position before any work is started.

When buying a property, it is imperative to consult your surveyors independent survey report as this will inform you of the modifications and changes that have previously been made at the property. Without this information your legal advisers would not be in a position to check whether or not the appropriate permissions were complied with and obtained.

Without your surveyors independent report, you could be left at risk if for example a wall or chimney breast may have been removed from the property and the remaining load above not properly supported. The likelihood of a future collapse would be a major risk to health and safety with additional cost implications and a negative impact on future saleability.

In some properties it might be the case that there is an unregulated extension which may have been in place for many years. If there is no obvious evidence of structural distress, you may be offered a form of insurance by your legal advisors called a warranty or indemnity insurance policy. This is in many cases not a solution as we have indicated elsewhere in this book. However, even if there is no obvious structural issue with such an extension it may have been constructed inadequately by current standards.

The classic situation we often see, is where an extension is built of what we call single skin or half brick construction. Single skin brick or block construction provides limited thermal capacity and has poor resistance to the passage of penetrating dampness. Such a form of construction would not comply with current regulations for use in habitable areas. This type of construction whether or not it has been in place for many years is not only inadequate because of the potential for dampness and condensation to penetrate but also performs very poorly in terms of its thermal capability.

The obvious effect is an increase to your fuel bills which is a particular concern at present with current fuel costs very high and expected to stay that way for the long term. Additionally, mortgageability may also be reduced due to this form of construction.

Another type of inadequate construction we often come across is low grade DIY style timber framed walls which in much the same way as you will see with single skin brick is often internally boarded and externally rendered. The external render would allow for a possibly mistaken belief by the untrained eye of appropriate construction.

Your surveyor should be experienced in looking for these types of hidden inadequacies and will accurately detail them in their independent report.

Another area where we frequently see DIY upgrades is when garages are internally lined with plasterboard or even thermal board and some form of raised timber floor is provided. The intention is to create an extra habitable room. Such modifications are often done by the owners themselves, with no technical guidance. It is not uncommon for a floating timber floor to have been installed without consideration of the need to protect the concealed framing timbers against damp rising through the concrete garage floor below, or whether proper ventilation is in place to guard against the risk of deterioration and decay.

This is why it is so important that whoever undertakes building works at the property, has in place a mechanism which can confirm that the works have been undertaken with technical capability and full regulatory compliance. But can there still be problems even when extensions have been constructed with appropriate planning and building regulation compliance?

Unfortunately, at yoursurveyors.com this is an issue we see on a regular basis. There are two particular situations which we see which will go on to create long term issues for the property.

A situation which we regularly see at your surveyors.com is where extensions between adjacent properties are constructed in such a way as to leave a very small gap between them, sometimes 300mm or even less. In consequence when the time comes for inevitable future maintenance on the extension side walls it is impossible to gain access because there is insufficient room to do so.

A problem with boundary issues may arise when extensions are constructed, perhaps by an over enthusiastic owner or builder who does not consider the top of the extension when they are working at the bottom. A situation can arise where, although the side walls of the extension may be appropriately within the boundaries of the subject property, when it comes to detailing the inevitable overhang of the roof tiling, eaves detailing and gutters, these will be encroaching over the boundary. It is imperative these situations are fully reported with any intending purchase so that the legal position can be satisfied prior to purchase commitment. If not, the buyer could be faced with very expensive works to redesign the structure to ensure the whole of the building is as it should be within the curtilage of the property on which the extension sits. This is yet another example of how your legal advisors would have no idea such a problem existed until it was pointed out to them by your surveyors.

Your surveyor's report is the only physical connection to the property which your legal advisors can have. Without this they would be unaware of present and future problems which could have a serious and expensive impact for your purchase, leaving you very much at risk.

A second situation we frequently see is in relation to loft conversions.

You will often see estate agent's details describing the area encompassed by modification of the roof structure as a "bonus room" or "loft area" or similar. This is sometimes an indication that nobody obtained permission before cutting and re-aligning elements of the structure of the roof frame. Many roof structures rely on angled struts supporting purlins which in turn support the rafters. These struts are frequently designed to carry the load of the roof down to a central spine wall which carries on down fully through the middle of the property.

A problem we often see at your surveyors.com is where people have decided they want some open space in the middle of the loft. In order to achieve this, they have removed the angled struts and replaced these with a series of vertical struts or even none at all. The result of this is that the whole load of the roof frame and coverings is redistributed to a completely different and inappropriate point and/or the roof frame is not adequately supported.

It is worth remembering that works of a structural character should be undertaken with regulatory compliance and generally calculated by a suitably qualified professional such as a Structural Engineer. They should never be estimated by a local builder or decided by the owner's choice of where they think the loads might now be carried and on what size of supporting structure.

Whether or not an additional room has been created in the roof space, modifying the structure of the roof does require regulatory compliance. Your legal advisors would rely on the information contained within your surveyor's independent survey report to inform their subsequent actions on your behalf.

We once inspected a three-year-old property with a style of roof constructed with modern trussed rafters.

There are inclined elements to each of the trusses which are integral to the continuing stability of the roof frame. However, the owner had decided that these were in the way because they wanted some additional storage space. The owner chose to cut away every single one of these integral structural members from every truss in the roof. How the whole framework and roof had not collapsed was a mystery to us, although it would just have been a matter of time before that would occur.

Extensions and modifications can certainly be a good thing and can add value to a property but as we have seen above, they can be fraught with issues from being poorly constructed or constructed without proper regulatory compliance. They can be constructed in a way which can damage other parts of the property. They can leave parts of the property at risk for the future due to poor consideration of the need for continuing maintenance and other issues.

There are many different ways in which people will choose to modify their home and quite often it is not until they come to sell the property that a professional company such as yoursurveyors.com is involved and anything which may not have been properly considered comes to light. The very important link between the property and the legal ramifications of these type of situations is your surveyor's independent report.

We are your professional, impartial eyes and ears and a direct link to your legal advisors.

BATS, RATS, DOGS AND CATS

Those plans you have for when you move into your new home could be thrown into chaos by nature. As well as plants that can potentially cause issues, there are many ways that animals in nature can disrupt your plans. Here we tell you about a few situations that as a buyer you may not be aware of until you get your surveyors to carry out a detailed, independent survey on your behalf.

Bats

In Britain all bat species and their roosts are legally protected by both domestic and international legislation.

This means you may be committing a criminal offence if you:
1. Deliberately take, injure, or kill a wild bat.

2. Intentionally or recklessly disturb a bat in its roost or deliberately disturb a group of bats.

3. Damage or destroy a place used by bats for breeding or resting (roosts) even if bats are not occupying the roost at the time.

4. Possess, advertise, sell, or exchange a bat of any species found in the wild in the EU whether dead or alive. All the above provisos would also pertain to the sale of body parts.

5. Intentionally or recklessly obstruct access to a bat roost.

Now, you may be thinking that bats are only found in the countryside or high up in the vaulted roofs of old derelict churches. The expression "bats in the belfry" is part of the reason why people think this. The truth however is very different.

Bats are fascinating animals; they are the only mammal with the ability to fly. There are over 1,400 species of bats in the world, and more are still being discovered. Bats account for more than a quarter of mammal species in the UK and around 20% of all mammal species worldwide. In the UK we have 18 species of bat. That is almost a quarter of our mammal species. For several weeks in summer, female bats gather in a maternity roost to have their young. In winter bats use hibernation roosts. Bats may also roost in bat boxes.

Bats are not rodents, and they don't nibble on wood, wires and other bits and pieces in buildings. However, the chances of a bat roost tucked away in a corner of the property you are thinking of buying is greater than you might expect.

A bat's habitat is known as its roost. Bats need different roosting conditions at different times of the year. Some bats prefer hollow trees, some like caves and some use both at different times. However, many bats shelter in buildings, behind hanging tiles and boarding or in roof spaces. UK bats do not construct roosts but use structures that are already available to them. That is why infrequently used parts of houses such as lofts, garages and outbuildings are so attractive to them. A roost is defined in law as any place a wild bat uses for shelter or protection. The number of bats does not matter. Neither do factors like the age of the building or how long the bats are likely to have been there. Every roost is important, and bats rely on a number of roosts in lots of locations if they are going to survive. Protecting the roost you found no matter the size is an important contribution to the conservation of bat populations.

It is important to be aware of the fact that they are a protected species and the implications of the legislation that is in place.

Sometimes bats can show up unexpectedly while building works are being carried out. If you or your contractors find a bat (or bats) during building work, you will need to follow these three steps:

1. Pause all works.

2. Make sure the bat is not in danger.

3. Seek advice about the works.

A roost is protected by law whether bats are present in it or not. There may be bats in other parts of the building too and work you do in another area may still cause disturbance and affect the roost. Any work in the building should be put on hold until further professional advice has been obtained. In most cases, you will be eligible for free advice from your Statutory Nature Conservation Organisation (SNCO). If the work is not eligible for free SNCO advice, the owner will need to hire an ecological consultant instead.

The Bat Conservation Trust are thanked for their assistance on the information herein.

Rodents

Mention the word rats and many people squeak themselves at the very thought. For some it conjures up images of sewers, disease and even the great plague of 1665. Whilst there are elements of truth in that, things have changed somewhat since then. Many people happily have rats as pets in their homes and they are very intelligent creatures. However, there are situations in which our furry companions can still be an unwanted guest.

The two main attractions that could entice rats and mice to take up residence in your house are food and shelter. If you do not tidy up properly and there is food waste on the floor or surfaces rodents are going to love it!

Rats and mice also need shelter, particularly during winter to avoid the worst of the cold.

So, how do rodents' get into your property?

A rat may climb up a rainwater pipe or a tree to reach your roof and then find its way in through a gap in a soffit board or an open window. Rats and mice can get in through open cellar access, missing air brick ventilator grills, or even through gaps in brickwork where old pipes have been removed and not made good afterwards.

Wild rats can also carry disease. These diseases can spread to people directly through the handling of rodents and contact with rodent faeces, urine, or saliva and eating food that has been contaminated with rodent waste or rodent bites.

Various diseases rodents can carry include:- Hantavirus, Leptospirosis, Lymphocytic Choriomeningitis (LCMV), Tularaemia and Salmonella.

Rats' love to chew, and this can cause serious damage to your property. Rats will chew through your collection of magazines or books, boxes filled with photographs, Christmas decorations and boxes of personal effects, electrical wires, plastics and more. Think of the damage that can be done to your storage in the roof space for example. Rats will chew water pipes. This is not simply because they are looking for water; it's because they have to. Their teeth grow continuously, and they need to chew constantly to keep them at a manageable length. A water pipe chewed through whilst you are asleep, or even worse on holiday could cause severe damage costing thousands to put right.

This is one of the reasons the water should be turned off when leaving your property empty for any period of time. It is not just pipes freezing and bursting which could cause water to cascade through your property damaging everything in its wake.

Rats' teeth are tough. Harder in fact than iron, platinum, and copper. When measured on the Mohs hardness scale, rats' teeth rank 5.5, Diamond is 10.

Your surveyors inspection will look for signs of rodent infestation. These are most commonly found in cellars, understairs cupboards, pantries or roof spaces. Such signs may include droppings, chewed material, or even traps and poison put down by the current or previous owners to try to eliminate the problem. We also suggest your solicitor's enquiries should include a question as to whether the current owners of the property have ever experienced issues with rodent infestation or whether any measures have ever been taken to try and eliminate this.

Dogs And Cats

So, let us now consider not just dogs and cats, but pets in general and not only from the personal perspective of having pets yourself. When buying a property any pets the current owners or their neighbours may have, ought to be considered before deciding whether or not to buy that property.

Pets are a great addition to a home and are ubiquitous across the nation. They teach children about love, care, and commitment. Whatever you are feeling and regardless of what may be happening, pets need to be looked after and in return they give so much. However, let's consider the situation when buying your new home. The current owners may have a dog or cat, something you did not realise as the pet was not there when you viewed the property. Your new neighbours may well have pets also. We often see signs of a pet in the property and can advise you on some of the issues this may bring to you after you move in.

Dogs and cats can carry infections such as, campylobacter infection, cat scratch disease, toxocariasis and toxoplasmosis.

Your surveyor will look for signs of faeces in gardens or sadly in some cases we have seen, even inside the property and warn you of these risks.

When considering your own pets, security is an important issue. What is the condition of the boundary markers which divide your land from adjacent land. For example, fencing and garden walls. Are the garden walls in a state of disrepair, could your pet escape from the garden? If this is the case then the costs of repair would need to be assessed.

In the short time spent viewing the property it is unlikely you would spend much of it in the garden. However, that would probably be your special private space in the summer months. Imagine the distress and frustration from realising your personal space has been invaded by your neighbours aggressive and noisy dogs.

Your surveyor will spend time outside, not only looking for problems with the outside of the building but also in the garden and outbuildings searching for faults and hazards. This allows ample time to assess the peaceful nature of the surrounding space which you will be able to factor into your purchasing decision.

Exotic Animals

Reptiles (including lizards, snakes, and turtles) and amphibians (including frogs, toads, and salamanders) are not recommended as pets for kids younger than 5 because of salmonellosis. This infection causes symptoms which can be more prevalent in young children.

Pet birds even if they are kept in a cage can also spread diseases such as cryptococcosis and psittacosis.

A deep clean of any new home is more important than ever when there have been pet birds there.

Although not a pet bird, evidence of the protected species House Martins at your property, which your surveyors would find and point out to you, also needs consideration. House Martins nests are commonly found underneath eaves and verge finishes. On rare occasions they can be found inside roof spaces or in sheds. They are colonial nesters, meaning they have an average group size of four to five nests. Larger colonies can be of groups of tens or even hundreds of nests. The nests may not be on one single property. It is often the case that nests are distributed over several properties that are grouped together.

House martins are fully protected under the Wildlife and Countryside Act 1981 which makes it an offence to kill, injure or take an adult bird, or to take, damage or destroy the eggs, young or nest of a house martin whilst it is being built or in use. Penalties that can be imposed for criminal offences in respect of a single bird, nest or egg contrary to the Wildlife and Countryside Act 1981 is an unlimited fine, up to six months imprisonment or both.

THE WORST ADVICE IN THE WORLD

Nothing seems to attract supposed experts who know very little quite like property. The one thing that links most of these "experts" is the fact that they either offer incorrect, inadequate, or partial and potentially damaging information which you should never act on.

There is a very good reason why residential surveyors take a very long time to become professionally qualified and then many years fine-tuning their knowledge and experience. There is a very good reason why they also have to undertake many hours of continuing professional development to maintain their professional qualifications and ensure they can offer correct professional advice in an ever-changing world.

Property is not straightforward even though many people think it is. Property is complex and buying any property without independent professional advice is very foolhardy.

Here at yoursurveyors.com we have inspected well over 30,000 residential properties and have over 50 years of experience and professional qualifications.

So, the next time you hear one of the following examples, make sure you do nothing until you have obtained your surveyor's independent survey report.

"My Friend / Dad / Partner / Mum / Cousin / Neighbour Is A Builder"

Indeed, any one of those people may be a very good builder with many years' experience of undertaking construction works and you would certainly expect they would have some knowledge of how properties are put together. Buying a new property doesn't need you to specifically understand how the property is put together, however, it is imperative you understand or can be advised about how all the elements of the property interact in usage. Also, what effect many different owners and years of occupation may have had upon the building and upon its original construction.

Having the admirable ability to construct a straight wall, plaster a room to an exquisite finish or pitch a roof, is not something to be sneered at. Certainly, most surveyors could not undertake any of those tasks. However, being able to construct a building to a professional standard does not give the builder the professional expertise to judge or consider cracks or movement in the property. A builder would not have the required level of professional qualification to understand which elements are and are not subject to mandatory regulatory compliance, nor are they likely to identify the signs or understand the huge difference between; xestobium rufovillosum or ernobius mollis, not to mention anobium punctatum. All are various forms of insect infestation which your surveyor is qualified to recognise, assess and advise you on.

In life, we all function with different skill sets for a reason. You wouldn't visit a cardiologist and ask them to remove your wisdom teeth. True, they are both involved in medicine but in very different ways.

Builders are experienced in construction but in a way that has little or no relevance to you in terms of the advice that you would need from your surveyor's independent survey report. A report which relies on skills acquired through many years of professional education and training. Most importantly, your surveyor's report is provided to you with a liability of competence upon which you can legally rely if any advice given to you is not up to standard. On the other hand, if your friendly builder gives you advice which turns out to be completely wrong, all the financial consequences which result from that will fall directly on yourself.

"Someone I Know Bought A House Nearby Just Last Year"

Another favourite.

When it becomes known that you are considering buying a property in a particular location you can be sure that if somebody within your circle purchased a property nearby recently, they will believe they have intimate knowledge of the local property market. Bolstered in this belief, they will feel the need to avail you of their advice concerning your property just because it's somewhere nearby or looks a bit similar.

The truth of the matter is they don't know any more about property now than they did before they purchased their property. Often, they will tell you in glowing terms how their property is lovely, but they did have trouble with the drains or the windows, or some of the fences were rotten, or there wasn't enough insulation in the loft.

All of which is completely irrelevant because every property is different. Not only in terms of how it's been originally put together, but, also, how it has been maintained over the years and what modifications have been made in that time. Who did the work, when and why and was it subject to the correct mandatory regulatory compliance. This comes under the heading of people who think they can acquire knowledge simply by association. It really doesn't work like that.

"I Know A Surveyor"

There are numerous surveyors in this country and a lot of confusion about their role. Generally, the only involvement people have with a surveyor is when moving home.

When instructing your surveyor's independent survey report, it is important you make sure that you are instructing a surveyor who is knowledgeable and experienced and specialises in residential survey work.

However, there are many, very different types of surveyors. A selection of these include:

    * Land Surveyor
    * Environmental Surveyor
    * Rural Practice Surveyor
    * Quantity Surveyor
    * Party Wall Surveyor
    * Boundary Surveyor
    * Planning and Development Surveyor
    * Valuation Surveyor
    * Commercial Surveyor
    * Residential Surveyor
    * Building Surveyor
    * Chartered Surveyor
    * Building Control Surveyor
    * Infrastructure Surveyor
    * Valuation Surveyor
    * Management Consultancy Surveyor
    * Geomatics Surveyor
    * Environmental Surveyor
    * Rural Surveyor
    * Timber and Damp Surveyor
    * Asbestos Surveyor

* Hydrographic Surveyor
* Minerals and Waste Surveyor
* Arts and Antiques Surveyor
* Facilities Management Surveyor

Just because somebody tells you they are a surveyor or they know a surveyor, it is highly likely that surveyor won't be the one best positioned to advise you, even casually about your intended property purchase.

Each of the above surveyors are trained in their own particular discipline which would not overlap with that of a residential surveyor who has been trained specifically to provide advice on property purchase. However, if approached for advice, perhaps on the recommendation of a friend, they will sometimes out of goodwill offer some advice. This may leave you with the impression that you have no need to instruct your own independent surveyor. Despite the good intentions of that person, what if their advice turns out to be incorrect or misleading?

The truth is, in much the same way as taking advice from other unqualified individuals, you will be left to pick up the bill. You can't go back to someone who gave you casual advice after the event and when defects and problems arise, complain that it was because of their advice that you are suffering loss, disturbance, and expense. This becomes even more embarrassing and upsetting if the individual concerned is part of your social circle or a friend.

It is imperative when buying property to instruct your own independent surveyor's report so you can get clear instructions and advice in black and white about the property, its pitfalls, and advantages and that you can rely on the qualifications and knowledge of the person undertaking the inspection.

Others Interpreting Your Independent Survey Report.

When you instruct your surveyor's independent survey report, part of the fee that you pay is to include as much after sales service conversation and explanation where relevant as needed.

Surveyor's reports are lengthy and technical documents probably including some terms with which you may be unfamiliar. The advice given by most surveyors is to read the report two or three times in order to fully digest its contents. Even after such careful reading, there may well be some elements of the report which warrant further explanation so you can fully consider your position in terms of moving forwards and negotiation. Remember, negotiation on the price cannot sensibly be finalised until such time as you know what you are actually buying and this can only be done once you know the full condition of the property. This will only be clear following your surveyor's independent survey inspection and report.

Bizarrely, we often hear of cases where prospective buyers take their survey report to the estate agent in order to seek clarity on some of the elements contained therein. The estate agent has a very important function in the sale process. They have a specific duty of care to achieve the best possible result for their client, the seller of the property. They can achieve this through marketing, designed to show the property in its best possible light and look to achieve the highest possible price they can on the sale.

Estate agents mostly do not carry the level of technical qualifications required to understand and interpret in detail independent survey reports. In fact, some might argue that it would be in their client's best interests if any concerns highlighted in the report could be reflected upon and considered in a way least likely to achieve a sale price reduction or in any way interrupt the progress of the sale.

Given that is in essence their duty of care to their client, the seller of the property, they are not best placed to be interpreting the survey report. This should only be done by the surveyor who undertook the inspection and with whom you as the purchaser have a direct client relationship.

Similarly, whilst sharing the content of your surveyor's independent survey report with family members and your own solicitor is usual practice, it is important that whatever guidance you are offered by those individuals should never take precedence over the specific interpretation of the report by the surveyor who undertook the inspection.

"The Mortgage Company Carries Out A Survey!"

This is probably one of the **worst** pieces of advice you will ever receive. We hope to make this message abundantly clear once and for all.

Mortgage companies send a valuer to undertake a valuation if you are lucky.

Nowadays it is much more likely that the valuation will be done remotely on a desktop basis and no professional will be sent to inpect the property at all.

This is referred to as a desktop valuation whereby a surveyor accesses up to date information online and calculates the valuation based on the available evidence usually following a comparable method.

There are also Automated Valuation Models (AVMS) which is similar to a desktop valuation but is often completely automated with little or no intervention. This is a service which combines mathematical or statistical modeling with databases of existing properties and transactions to calculate property values. The majority of AVMs compare similar properties sold at the same point in time.

Drive-by appraisals are another alternative that lenders instruct. Instead of a valuer or surveyor inspecting both the inside and outside, they only examine the outside and available online information to compile the valuation.

None of these options provide an in depth analysis of the buildings condition whatsoever.

In cases where the mortgage company do send a valuer or surveyor to inspect the property, they will still not undertake a full survey and the average difference in inspection time is around two to three hours.

They will undertake a valuation only and the client for that valuation is not you, it is the lender. Do not allow anybody to try to convince you that a valuation for the lender is a survey. This has never been true and it never will be true.

Under no circumstances should you ever rely on a valuation which is done without a proper inspection of the property, and with the lender as the client, as your safeguard when buying a property. The only sensible way to buy a property is after you have directly instructed your own surveyor's independent survey report.

"Old Houses Are Built Better."

This is one of the most popular urban myths. In reality, there is good and bad across every spectrum of age and type of property. Generally, in their natural state, older houses tend to be less environmentally friendly and thermally efficient than their more modern counterparts when we consider fuel costs, the impact of heating and lighting and the effects of climate change more than we did before.

Old Victorian houses would have been constructed with no

insulation, draughty windows, timber ventilated floors and often solid walls. Modern equivalents typically, have cavity wall construction with insulation integrated into the walls, solid floors reducing draughts and significant levels of insulation as a requirement in roof spaces, along with double glazing and the like. They may even include other features such as air source or ground source heat pumps or solar panels.

That is not to say that you cannot make improvements in most of these areas on older houses to bring them up to a more modern specification. It is true that as a general rule, older houses will have shallower foundations than more modern properties and shallower foundations can increase the susceptibility to structural movement due to varying ground conditions beneath these shallow elements. However, we have a vast selection of older properties throughout this country some dating from many hundreds of years ago. Whilst construction styles and standards have almost inevitably varied and improved over the years, it would be very unfair to dismiss the quality of older properties, many of which, let's not forget, have survived two world wars throughout their life.

Every property should be considered on its merits and your surveyor's independent survey report will bring to your attention anything which is relevant including the sometimes very differing issues which occur in modern properties compared to the older buildings.

Be careful not to take the worst advice in the world.

ABOUT THE AUTHORS

ZOE BAKER – MANAGING DIRECTOR & FOUNDER

Zoe Baker started her working life at 15 years old as a trainee hairdresser. She progressed and by 21 she was a Senior Stylist however, she was changing and developing as a person and wanted a new challenge. She got a job at a chartered surveyors working in the admin team. Little did she know, she had developed a plethora of transferrable skills from her years in the hairdressing industry which drove her forward into her journey in the property industry.

She fell in love with the surveying profession and progressed to a manging position within 2 years. She is the surveying operations guru and has learnt, mastered and automated every process that contributes to running a surveying business.

In 2020, Zoe completed her SAVA qualification and obtained her Royal Institution of Chartered Surveyors accreditation where she is an associate member. She then set up her own residential surveying business yoursurveyors.com which is a technologically focused, customer service driven and forward thinking company where she specialises in pre purchase Level 2 and 3 surveys and valuations on residential properties for the public and has been named in numerous 5-star reviews that the company has received. Zoe is well-known for her passion for the profession and constantly looking at ways to improve her business with her clients' needs and requirements at the forefront.

Zoe's journey is unique, and she is extremely passionate about surveying and service delivery and enjoys running her own business as she gets to be creative and build her own empire.

Zoe won "RICS Residential Surveyor of the Year 2022" award which was the cherry on top of the cake that she has been baking for almost 10 years in the surveying profession.

GARRETT O'HANLON – TECHNICAL DIRECTOR

Garrett O'Hanlon qualified as a chartered surveyor in 1983 and since that time has specialised in residential survey and valuation work. He is a Fellow of the Royal Institution of Chartered Surveyors, with 40 years' experience of inspections ranging through mortgage and private valuations, homebuyer reports, building surveys and defect inspections.

He has inspected over 30,000 residential properties ranging across all types from 15th century barns and farmhouses to sections of converted castles, and of course the usual more modern traditional houses, bungalows, and flats.

Garrett has employed and personally trained over 50 Chartered Surveyors and was part of the official Royal Institution of Chartered Surveyors team responsible for producing the widely recognised "Royal Institution of Chartered Surveyors level 2 homebuyers report".

As a professional mentor to Zoe Baker, he was delighted to see her not only go on to qualify professionally under his mentorship, but then go on to achieve national recognition and become winner of the "RICS Young Residential Surveyor of the Year 2022" award.

For around two years he was a frequent panellist on a show on Sky television called "Property Question Time" in which he and other property experts answered questions from the public.

ACKNOWLEDGEMENT

Our friends, families, colleagues and clients.

hoa.org.uk
architectscertificate.co.uk
nfrc.co.uk
property-care.org
gift-a-tree.com
unbiased.co.uk
Nhsinform.Scot
Thames water
gassafetycerts.com
niceic.com
ukradon.org
The bat conservation trust
discoverwildlife.com
kidshealth.org
rspb.org.uk
arca.org.uk

Printed in Great Britain
by Amazon

44327999R00086